"EmailDelive
Prese

MW00973344

Heather Seitz'

"The Experts Guide to Email Marketing:

How to Avoid the Top 12 Email Marketing Mistakes That

Prevent Your Emails from Getting to the Inbox"

Copyright Information

Limits of Liability / Disclaimer of Warranty:

The authors and publisher of this book and the accompanying materials have used their best efforts in preparing this program. The authors and publisher make no representation or warranties with respect to the accuracy, applicability, fitness, or completeness of the contents in this program. They disclaim any warranties (expressed or implied), merchantability, or fitness for any particular purpose.

The authors and publisher shall in no event be held liable for any loss or other damages, including but not limited to special, incidental, consequential, or other damages. As always, the advice of a competent legal, tax, accounting, or other professional should be sought. The authors and publisher don't warrant the performance, effectiveness or applicability of any sites listed in this book. All links are for information purposes only and are not warranted for content, accuracy or any other implied or explicit purpose.

The authors and publisher make no income claims, promises, predictions or guarantees are made of any kind. Any reference or income examples are exceptional results, which do not apply to the average person and are not intended to represent or guarantee that anyone will achieve the same or similar results.

This manual contains material protected under International and Federal Copyright Laws and Treaties. Any unauthorized reprint or use of this material is prohibited.

Table of Contents

Your Personal Invitation from Heather Seitz

Because you've purchased "The Experts Guide to Email Marketing: How to Avoid the Top 12 Email Marketing Mistakes That Prevent Your Emails from Getting to the Inbox," it proves to me that you're serious about your email program and want to have a bigger, more responsive list that opens your messages, clicks on your links, and buys your products and services.

I'd like to invite you to get your own Email Marketing Audit, where my team will go through your email program and show you which of these mistakes you may be making and how to correct them. As added value, we'll also add you to our weekly "Email Delivered Tips" Newsletter that shares with you the latest information on email marketing and email deliverability as we learn about it.

If you want to identify potential problems in your email program, increase your open rates and click through rates, and increase your sales through email marketing, then here's what I'd like to invite you to do:

1. Go ahead and logon to **www.EmailDelivered.com/audit** and sign up for a free audit. It takes about 60 seconds and will save you time and money, and will keep you from continuing to play the guessing game with your email marketing. This could be the single best business decision you make all year.

2. Again, signing up is easy and the audit is FREE for people that purchased this book. Just go to **www.EmailDelivered.com/audit** and sign up for a free account. We promise not to spam you or share your information with anyone...

About the Author

Heather Seitz is the co-founder of EmailDelivered, a concierge email marketing service that provides marketers a one-of-a-kind solution to their email marketing program.

She and her husband - and business partner - built the company from the ground up. Heather started marketing and selling products online back in 2002 in the real estate industry. She ran that business successfully for the next 10 years, largely through email marketing. In that time, she personally sent out thousands of campaigns to tens of thousands of subscribers each and every week.

Back in 2006, something changed, and her results weren't what they used to be. Before ditching her entire business, she took the advice of a well-known marketer at the time and moved her email program to a new solution. Instantly, she saw her profits rebound. In fact, the very next month, she increased her bottom line by 560%.

Shortly thereafter, she ran into some roadblocks with her email marketing again! Without an email service provider to contact, she was forced to figure it out on her own. They teamed up with an insider at an ISP to not only solve her own delivery problems, but to create a service that is now used by the most successful online marketers and business owners.

Heather has the unique ability to combine her extensive background in email marketing (from the marketer's viewpoint) with the technical side of email, the part that gets your emails to the inbox. Since she has perspective of both sides, she has been able to continue to grow and expand the company, helping deliver 100s of millions of emails each and every month for her clients and customers.

Her ability to understand the needs of marketers and the requirements of the ISPs makes her a unique resource for businesses of all sizes.

Bottom Line: Heather helps real business owners, just like you, take the guesswork out of email marketing and take back control over their email so they can focus on what they do best: sell products and services.

For speaking or consulting inquiries, or to get updates on email marketing, email deliverability and email trends, you can contact Heather through her website at http://www.HeatherSeitz.com.

Introduction

Welcome to "The Experts Guide to Email Marketing: How to Avoid the Top 12 Email Marketing Mistakes that Prevent Your Emails from Getting to the Inbox." With 8+ years of working with top email marketers, and over 13 years of firsthand experience with email marketing and email deliverability in my own business, I have personally seen and/or made each and every one of these mistakes AND know how to help YOU avoid them in the future.

I started marketing via email back in 2001 and didn't have a clue. I made a LOT of mistakes during that time, and a few major ones, which led me down the path of creating one of the most respected email companies in the marketplace.

I was fortunate, early on, to bring on an industry insider (an email administrator at an ISP). This is one of the guys who determines whether or not our email messages make it to the inbox, get sent to the spam folder, or blocked at the source. As a result, I learned a whole lot about the "technical" side of email. That's the part that most Internet marketers **NEVER** learn. I have also been fortunate to be on the cutting edge of what's coming down the pike since the ISPs know what's going on before the rest of us do!

What I am about to teach you in the following pages is based on both my own experience and that of working with marketers over the years. I've had an eyewitness view to see the cumulative effect of these mistakes over literally BILLIONS of email messages sent.

This isn't theory. This isn't opinion. The pages that follow will cover many of the mistakes that I see over and over, how to avoid those mistakes, and to provide you with solid email **marketing** tips that will make a tremendous difference in your email marketing.

I can almost guarantee that you are currently making one or more of the mistakes discussed in this book. And I can also guarantee that 99% of all email marketers simply aren't aware of many of the mistakes in here. They're not the sort of things you hear about in courses, training classes, or even from masterminds, and certainly not from your email service provider. Email service providers have a vested interest in making sure you DON'T know a lot of this since it only makes their job harder!

People simply don't know what they don't know. As such, **it's not your fault if you're making these mistakes.**

If you're brand new to email, you'll learn some things that will help you start on the right foot and avoid a lot of costly mistakes in the long run, and if you're a seasoned veteran, chances are you'll uncover some things you weren't aware of and will be able to see some immediate changes as you implement the fixes I cover.

How Is This Book Different From Any Other Book on Email Marketing

The difference between this book and other books on the topics of either email marketing or email deliverability is that I have PERSONAL experience on both sides of the fence... As an email marketer, sending out 2-3 emails a day for the better part of ten years AND as a service provider handling the technical aspects of email marketing, managing relationships with ISPs, and getting emails to the inbox (and all the stuff that goes along with that).

Most books written on email marketing cover very little - if anything - on deliverability and how the two work together. Most books written on the technical aspects of email are simply too boring or geared strictly for tech-heads, that the average marketer simply glazes over after the first 3 sentences and gives up.

Authors tend to be EITHER marketers OR technical folks, so the information is generally missing half of the puzzle. In this book, you get insight from both the marketer viewpoint and how the ISPs see your emails.

Disclaimer

Email is a moving target. There are lots of players in the field, some better than others.

In this book, I've specifically opted NOT to mention any providers by name. Samples and case studies are just that and are not meant to highlight any particular provider. I have also specifically stayed away from any types of income claims because each and every situation is different. I cannot make any promises that following any or all of the advice in this book will change your life!

If you're looking for a magic bullet, and a free pass to the inbox, this book is not for you. This book is designed to arm you with the information that you need to be successful with your email marketing and to share with you some tools and resources.

What We'll Cover

We're going to talk about the biggest mistakes people make with email marketing that are hurting not only your deliverability, but also your bottom line. Happy subscribers = more money in your bank account.

We will cover the following topics:

- What your email reputation is and why it's important

- The role of content in your email messages

- How to minimize the number of people that click the "spam" button (and why this is super important)

- The keys to re-engaging your subscribers, and why you should be doing this regularly

- The right way to participate in product launches and affiliate offers to ensure that your email reputation doesn't get damaged

- Why list hygiene is important and how to take control over your own list

- The proper way to build a list (and common strategies that can destroy your email program instantly.)

- How to strike a balance between content and sales messages

- How to set proper expectations up front and stick to them while providing a positive experience for your subscribers

- Why you need to get a mobile strategy in place (and easy things you can do to optimize for mobile)

- How your current email service may be sabotaging your marketing

- And more...

We'll even take a moment towards the end to cover the technical stuff that nobody really "wants" to know about, but really is important!

Biggest Email Marketing Mistake

The biggest email marketing mistake that I see people make is simply turning over their email program to an email service provider and not paying any attention to what's going on.

It's easy to assume that since you're paying a service to get your emails delivered to the inbox, that's what's happening. However, even providers that claim 99% deliverability are not telling you the whole story.

And because the industry makes more money by keeping their customers less educated, most marketers don't even know what they don't know.

While I understand you may not WANT to necessarily learn all this stuff, if you don't... then you'll be losing money. PERIOD.

But don't worry! I'm going to make this simple for you and check the super technical stuff at the door.

Why This Is Important

This is important for a number of reasons.

When it comes to selecting the right email service provider or infrastructure for your email, it's never too late to make a change (and get things setup the right way).

You see, when you're not paying attention, your results can begin to suffer. You may see a slow decline in open rates or clicks or you may see a drastic drop overnight.

When this happens, you've got to know WHY and what you can do about it before it's too late.

What This Means

All this means is that you will now have CONTROL over your email marketing and you won't be "hoping" you're getting the right answers from your ESP. If you've ever tried to call into your ESP (email service provider) when you suspect a problem, chances are you're greeted with a customer support person that really can't provide you with REAL answers.

Worst- case scenario, they try to upsell you into some "package" that they can help you with your content. Most likely, they simply tell you to fix your content.

But... there's a lot more to the story that they're not telling you. The rep on the phone doesn't actually have the ability to dig further, so you're stuck accepting their answer or making a change to a new email solution where you DO have visibility and the ability to get the important information.

You see, there IS a lot more that can be done to track down the root of the problem, but if they did that, it could expose more problems and cause headaches for them. And by the nature of how they're setup, they're just not going to provide the information you're wanting or needing.

Penalties for NOT Doing This

Ultimately, by not maintaining control of your email along with a certain amount of knowledge, you're literally throwing money down the drain. You are losing contact with your subscribers, losing sales, and ultimately harming your business.

It costs a lot to get new subscribers whether you're using PPC advertising or affiliates to drive leads to your website, and you should do everything you can to maintain the relationship as long as possible (assuming they still WANT to receive your emails, of course).

The Mistakes (& Fixes)

The good news is that few people know the things that we're going to cover in this book. And most of those that do have a vested interest in NOT sharing the information with you. Once you're armed with the information, and able to take the right actions, you'll be able to beat out your competition every time.

That means more money from product launches. That means more money from affiliate promos. That means more money from your own sales. And so on...

Plus, you'll have more control and visibility into what's going on with your email, and the ability to make changes when necessary without derailing your entire program or having to start from scratch.

With that... let's go ahead and dive on in.

Mistake #1: Not Knowing What Your Email Reputation Is
(Reputation is Everything)

At the heart of your email program lies your reputation. You may or may not have heard about email reputation before, so we'll take a moment to make an analogy to a credit rating, if you will, for your email.

Just like with your personal credit, there are a number of different ways this information is reflected. For example, if you have items in collections, a foreclosure, and a bankruptcy in your recent credit history, you're not going to be looked upon favorably when you try to borrow money.

The way that institutions gather information ABOUT you is through a credit report from one of the 3 major reporting services or through FICO (if they are simply looking for a numeric score). The thing to keep in mind is that your credit RATING/score is due to the items in your file, not the other way around.

Your email reputation is similar in many ways in that there are a number of factors that determine whether or not the ISPs (i.e. Gmail, Hotmail, AOL, Yahoo, etc.) view your emails favorably. If not, they may block your message entirely. This is like being denied a home loan. Or they may let the message in and send it to the spam folder. Think of this like getting approved for a home loan, but having to pay 11% interest instead of 4%.

In the latter example, your credit isn't dismal, but it isn't very good either!

We'll cover a few tools you can use to check your reputation shortly, but let's start by talking about what makes up your "email reputation" in the first place. There a number of things that determine your reputation and how the ISPs perceive your email program. The top factors include:

- General setup/configuration (do you have all the technical pieces in place)?

- List quality

- Spam traps

- Complaints / Complaint Rate

- Message content

Your email reputation is tied not only to your IP address, but also to your domain, with the domain becoming more and more important.

The problem here is that MOST marketers and online business owners really don't know much about this, and it's one of THE most important pieces of the email deliverability puzzle. If your email doesn't make it to the inbox, the rest doesn't matter. Here's a breakdown of the critical elements that make up your reputation.

IP Reputation

First things first... If the concept of an IP address is new to you, imagine a funnel. The mail all goes in to the top of the funnel and goes out through the narrow part of the funnel. That narrow part is your IP address.

In a clean funnel, all the mail goes through.

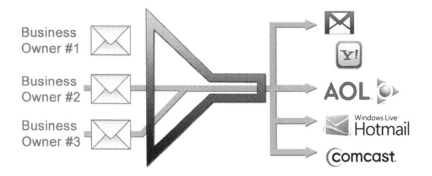

However, if someone causes the funnel to get clogged, if you will, then mail to one or more ISPs may get blocked for everyone sending through the funnel, or IP address.

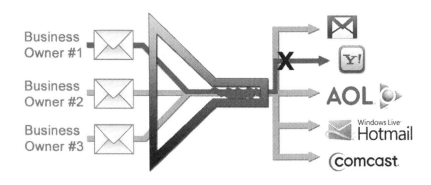

If you're using a typical email service provider (ESP), you're sharing one or more IP addresses with hundreds, possibly THOUSANDS of other marketers. There are a couple of inherent problems with this:

Your **IP reputation is only as good as the worst marketer in the group**.

Because of #1, the ESPs often impose very strict and rigid rules on you that are above and beyond any ISP best practices.

You never know the truth when it comes to what's going on with your email when you use a traditional ESP.

In other words, you may get virtually zero complaints, but if someone else using the same resources is getting a LOT of complaints on the IP address(es), then he/she could be causing your emails to get sent to the spam folder, or worse, rejected altogether.

There is a tool that you can use to get a general idea of your IP reputation called Sender Score. Here's a screen shot of one of our dedicated IPs/domains:

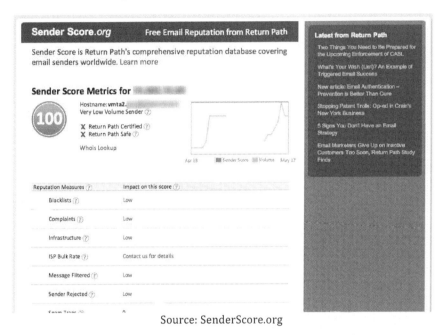

Source: SenderScore.org

The higher the number, the better. But, it is important to understand that just because you may have a high number, it doesn't mean that your emails are getting delivered to the inbox. This is just kind of a snapshot of the overall health of your email program in a single moment in time. It doesn't take into account history.

Also, not all ISPs report their data to Sender Score, nor do all providers collect or use data from Sender Score. Having said that, it can be a helpful tool to initially evaluate potential problems with your email program.

You also have to take into account the reputation of the domain.

Domain Reputation

Previously, ISPs relied almost entirely on the reputation of the IP address. Since that's relatively easy for spammers to game, more and more ISPs are now ALSO relying on the reputation of actual domains. The tricky part here is that there are often multiple domains in a given email and each has a potential impact on what happens to your email message(s).

When we refer to domains, we're not ONLY referring to the domains that you use in your message content, but also the "from" address, the "reply to" address, and unsubscribe/tracking URLs.

Some URLs may not even be visible unless you look at the email source. With most email clients, you'll have control over your from email address and with many, you'll have control over the reply to address. But rarely will you have any way to change the return-path or the domains used in tracking/unsubscribe links.

Let's take a moment to go over the different types of domains and how they impact your message delivery.

Domains in the Message Body

These are the domains to which you are sending your traffic. In other words, they click on a link in your email and are sent to a page on the web. Even if you're using tracking links or redirects, the landing page has an impact.

From Address

This is the email address that people see in the "from" section of the email. It may look something like: Heather Seitz <heathers-address-that-shows-in-the-mail-client@emaildelivered.com>. This is also the one that you ask people to "whitelist," if you're offering those instructions at the point of opt-in or at some time during your marketing funnel.

Reply To Address

This is the email address that any replies will go to. This may or may not be the same as the "from" address, depending on the email software/service that you are using.

Return-Path

The problem comes into play when the return path address has deliverability problems. Recently, there was a well-known ESP that had built a poor reputation for their return path domain. As a result, ALL of their customers were having issues getting their email to the inbox.

In fact, as a result, we had a client come over to EmailDelivered from this provider, and her open rate increased 42% overnight *(because the messages were getting to the inbox)*.

NOTE: With a traditional email service provider, you will have zero control over the return path. This is set up and controlled by the provider.

Unsubscribe/Tracking URLs

These are all the links used for tracking clicks, opens, and processing unsubscribe requests. Generally, these are not changeable. Therefore, if any of these domains are on a blacklist, or even a greylist, they can have an impact on your deliverability.

There's a well known CRM system that is constantly on and off blacklist services, such as URIBL and ALL of their tracking links contain this URL, which is a problem for obvious reason! (Every email sent out of this system is sending emails with greylisted or blacklisted URLs).

To see all of the domains in your email message, you can view the original email source. This is handled differently in each email client so you'll want to look up how to view the source in the particular email provider that you are using.

This will look similar to HTML code if you were to view the source of a website.

Here's an example of how you'd find this in Gmail:

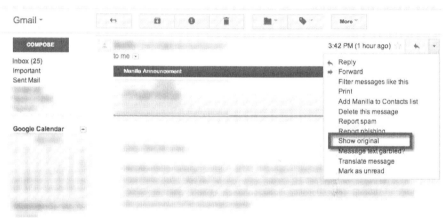

So How Does My Reputation Really Impact My Email Deliverability

Here are some real world problems that are a result of reputation issues including the domain, the IP or a combination of both.

- Open rates are declining (either slowly over time or drastically in a short period of time)

- Clicks and sales are dropping

- Messages go "missing" and your ESP can't tell you where they are

- It takes hours for your emails to get delivered

- Increased bounces

The first two bullet points are fairly straightforward. If mail isn't making it to the inbox, fewer people will see your emails. Therefore, fewer people will open your messages, and obviously your clicks and sales will drop.

But, the next three points are where things get a little more "gray". So let's go ahead and take a closer look at these items.

1. Messages go "missing" and your ESP can't tell you where they are

Let's say you send out an email. It never arrives in your inbox, so you check your spam folder. And it never arrives in your spam folder.

So you pick up the phone and call your email service provider (or open a ticket) and they ultimately tell you that a certain percentage of all email just goes "missing".

Well, that's *really* not the case, ESPECIALLY when we're talking about reputable services like Gmail, Yahoo, Hotmail, etc.

There are a number of points at which an email can be tracked: When the message leaves your software, when it arrives at the mail transport agent, when it leaves the mail transport agent, and so on. Very rarely does it just "disappear." In almost all cases, it is possible to track a message from the time it leaves your email software until it is delivered or bounced.

What happens more often than not, is the ESP has simply deleted the mail for one reason or another. This may happen in a case where the queues get so large, that the mail gets backlogged and they choose to delete it rather than have mail delayed by days.

The IP address might be blocked by an ISP and the email service provider decides to delete the queue rather than delay messages for hours, or even days in some cases. And the list goes on.

The point is, very rarely does mail just go "missing."

2. It Takes Hours for Your Emails to Get Delivered

Let's say you send an email and it ultimately DOES get delivered (whether it be the inbox or the spam folder) 12 hours later.

Without getting too technical, one of two things is happening. (1) Your mail is getting stuck in a queue behind other senders. If there are too many senders, it could take hours to get out or (2) If you've got a poor reputation (for any of the reasons mentioned at the beginning of this chapter), they may choose to throttle your messages.

What this means is that they are only letting a certain number of emails through each hour. So, normally, they may allow 10,000 per hour, but because of certain reputation issues, they're allowing a tiny fraction of that.

Add "missing" messages and "delays" together and it's a recipe for email disaster, especially if you're promoting a time sensitive event like a teleseminar, webinar, or product launch.

3. Increased Bounces

I don't want to bore you with all the "tech geek" speak (you can Google "rfc email" if you want some 'light' reading!).

There are a number of reasons that an email message might bounce.

It's important to know the details about the types of bounces you're receiving. If you're receiving a lot of "technical" or "IP block" bounces, it indicates that there is some sort of reputation problem. Either the ISP is rejecting your emails entirely or they're throttling your emails.

For example, Hotmail may not "block" your IP address entirely, but they <u>may</u> limit how much mail you can send through per hour. As such, the mail gets backed up. The queue fills up and eventually the messages are dumped or bounced.

The level of detail you'll receive about bounces varies depending on the service that you're using. For instance, with EmailDelivered, we break it down into 10 categories that are easy to understand. Other ESPs will show you hard bounces, soft bounces, and technical bounces only, without any specific detail as to what the real reason for the bounce is.

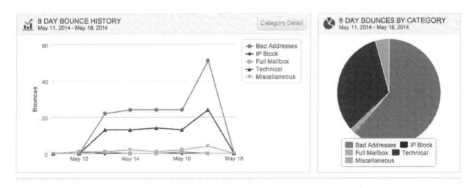

In a nutshell, if there is any sort of reputation issue with either your IP address or sending domain, you can find yourself having deliverability problems.

Ultimately, you need to pay attention to your email reputation, both the IP address and the domains. Regardless of whether or not you're using an email service provider or hosting the email on your own server, it is your responsibility to know what exactly is going on with your reputation.

If you're using an email service provider with shared IPs, you'll have little ability to influence the reputation, but you can hold your ESP accountable and you can keep an eye on the domains that you do have control over.

Remember, you're only as good as the weakest link on the service. This is one of the reasons they impose such strict rules like forced double opt-in, not permitting list uploads, and so on.

Reputation is the basis for everything else that we're going to cover over the next pages.

Throughout the remaining chapters of this book, we're going to cover a number of topics that will determine whether your emails make it to the inbox and how to keep your subscribers engaged with your emails. We'll go into greater detail on topics such as:

- **Message content** and how it plays a part in sending your email to the spam folder or delivering it to the inbox.

- Why people hit the "spam button" and how you can **minimize the complaints** you get.

- Why you may see a drop in open rates and click through rates and what you can do to keep those metrics up.

- How **affiliate marketing and product launches** can hurt your deliverability and damage your relationship with your subscribers - *and what you can do to insulate yourself from problems.*

- Why **list hygiene** is the death of your email program and how to perform list hygiene the RIGHT way (and not lose active subscribers).

- **List building practices** that can damage your reputation from the start.

- The key to **balancing sales messages with content** and why this protects your reputation.

- The right - and wrong - way to market to your list by setting expectations up front and segmenting subscribers.

- **Mobile marketing** and what you need to be doing now to ensure that you're making the most out of your campaigns.

- The **technical stuff** that you probably don't want to think about, but that you need to know if you want to reach your subscribers.

- Why using a shared IP can cost you thousands (or more)

- The main thing you need to know is that you do have an email reputation with the ISPs and it's your job to keep that reputation as clean as possible.

5 Key Chapter Takeaways

1. Everyone has a specific email reputation and it's important to monitor yours regularly and keep it as clean as possible.

2. The top factors that impact your email reputation are general setup/configuration, list quality, spam traps, complaints/complaint rate, and message content.

3. If you're using an ESP (email service provider) with shared IP addresses, you are only as good as the weakest link.

4. Not all domains are visible in your emails. It's important to know - and test - all the domains in your emails (and your headers).

5. Messages don't just "disappear". Generally, when a message seems to vanish, it is due to a problem with the reputation.

In the next chapter, we're going to go cover the role of IP addresses in more detail and discuss shared IPs versus dedicated IPs.

Mistake #2: Using Shared IP Addresses to Send Your Email *(You're Only As Good As the Weakest Link)*

As you know by now, reputation is critical when it comes to getting your email messages delivered to the inbox. And while there are several components that make up your reputation, the IP address is one of the most important pieces of the reputation puzzle.

What Exactly IS An IP Address and Why Does It Matter with Email?

You can think of an IP address as the funnel that gets your email out, or a pipe if you will. All of your email messages have to go through that "pipe" in order to get to your subscribers' inboxes.

If anything happens to that pipe or funnel, your deliverability can be compromised, which in turn causes your messages to get sent to the spam folder or, worse, rejected at the source.

Types of IP Addresses

When it comes to email, there are basically 2 scenarios when it comes to IP addresses.

1. Shared

2. Dedicated

Dedicated IP addresses are certainly preferred, and you'll see why in a moment. However, there are times when using shared IPs might make sense.

Shared IPs

Generally, you're going to be "sharing" IP addresses when you're using an Email Service Provider.

You simply sign up for an account, login, and you're off to the races.

This is great if you're just getting started and need to focus on other aspects of your business. Email will be but one component of your business early on and you'll have lots of other tasks and projects to focus your attention.

Solutions that offer shared IPs tend to be inexpensive when you've got a small list. It's a great way to build a list from scratch so you can focus on the rest of your business. You probably won't have significant delivery issues and you are probably not mailing out as many offers if you're just getting started either. It's better to use your resources to build your list and build your foundation.

On the flip side, there are often very strict rules. As you build a bigger list, this can become problematic. I'd say about 20% of the people come over to us because their email service provider has threatened to shut down their account.

The funny thing is… that those customers that come over generally have really good list practices, and tend to be some of our best types of customers. In fact, one customer was shut off from their CRM instantly, and when they came over to EmailDelivered, they routinely saw open rates of 30% or greater. That's with a list of over 250,000 subscribers!

The reason that email service providers don't want these folks is because they represent a higher risk. There are certain thresholds that ISPs have for things such as bad addresses, complaints, and so on, before it starts to impact your delivery.

As a result, the ISPs are even more strict in order to make sure that no single customer poisons the pool.

Just because you follow "best practices" doesn't mean that you don't represent a risk to the email service providers.

The one important thing that you need to know about shared IPs is that you are only as good as the worst person sharing those IPs with you.

In the last chapter, we made the analogy comparing your email sender reputation to your credit rating.

Well, imagine for a moment that you had to share your personal credit score with other people, and that you have absolutely NO control over with whom you share that score? In other words, you could be forced to share an IP (or pool of IP addresses) with someone that has the equivalency of a bankruptcy and 5 delinquent credit cards.

Regardless of how good your credit behavior is, it doesn't matter because the other sender is hurting YOUR reputation.

This is essentially how shared IP addresses work. In other words, if you're using an Email Service Provider with shared IPs, you are absolutely sharing the reputation with everyone else using that IP (or pool of IPs).

By the way... If you're the guy - or gal - with the equivalent of an email "bankruptcy", then a dedicated IP just might not be for you!

Dedicated IPs

In a dedicated environment, you have total control over your email program. As long as you follow the ISP best practices, you should be successful. You can remove the extra layer that the email service provider lays on top of the ISP requirements.

You'll still be required to follow CAN-SPAM and best practices as defined by the ISPs. You still can't send spam. You'll also have your hosting provider terms of service to adhere to.

You'll still have some rules, but I would venture to say that if you're reading this, then you're probably trying to do the right things already and simply need a little help from time to time to manage things.

Once you've got a list of over 15,000 and you're mailing pretty frequently, you'll want to consider looking at solutions that offer you a dedicated IP address. It simply gives you more control, more flexibility, and better overall deliverability.

Which Option Should I Choose?

When it comes to email, you basically have 2 choices:

1. A shared IP address on an ESP (email service provider)

2. A dedicated IP address over which you have total control.

Ideally with #2, you have control over everything including the domain, return path, etc.

We've already mentioned the potential problems with a shared IP address. This is one of the reasons that ESPs are so strict with their rules and regulations and are quick to kick people off. One bad apple can spoil the bunch.

And your email program is only as good as the worst sender in that shared range.

In almost all cases, email service providers operate with shared IP addresses. They're simply not in the "individual IP address" space. It takes more work to manage 1000 different customers on dedicated IPs than it does to strictly police all the users sharing the same handful of IP addresses. If something goes wrong with one IP, they can shut it off and send through the others until they fix the problem.

They can also kick off offenders instantly.

However, in 95% of cases, I've found that people WANT to do the right things when it comes to their email, and these ESPs simply don't take the time – or provide the assistance - to help them do that.

With a dedicated IP address, you're generally going to have a piece of software that you can purchase off the shelf (like Interspire Email Marketer, arpReach, Oempro, or other similar off-the-shelf solutions). You then use this email software to send through your own IP address.

Do keep in mind that you certainly still have to comply with the terms of service of your hosting provider or IP provider.

NOTE: You can use the IP address from your hosting provider or use an "SMTP relay service" such as EmailDelivered, who understands email and what you're trying to do and tends to be more willing to work with you when issues arise.

It's YOUR own email pipe, if you will.

You obviously can't send spam.

You still shouldn't purchase lists.

All the common sense stuff still applies! But you CAN have total control over who is using that IP address to send email and what types of messages are sent THROUGH that IP.

You're the only one that has an impact on the reputation of that IP address.

This is almost ALWAYS a positive provided that you're running a solid email program. However, if you're the kind of person sending affiliate network offer, after affiliate network offer, over, and over again, there could be some issues. (You might be one of those that are hurting the reputation of other senders ;-))

Now I'm not suggesting you can't send out offers using these networks, just do it the "right" way, and balance it with the rest of your program.

The bottom line is that if you have a list of 15,000 or more, and are sending out at least 2 email promotions per week, then it's time to start looking at a dedicated IP solution for your email program. The slight increase in cost will easily generate more revenue for you, often with your very first campaign. (See Chapter 6: "The Lazy Affiliate")

There are several solutions to get this setup, but it's important that you do it the right way from the get go (See Chapter 12: The Foolish Man Builds His House on Sand!). You'll want to make sure all of this is setup for you from the ground up BEFORE you start mailing.

There are really only 3 steps to getting this done:

1. Install email software on your server

2. Make sure you have a dedicated IP address (there are solutions like EmailDelivered that will allow you to use an external dedicated IP address or you can use the IP address at your hosting provider, assuming they allow bulk email marketing).

3. Watch your reputation (All of the things covered in this book will help you with this piece).

NOTE: If you want to set it and forget it, EmailDelivered has an all-in-one plan that will handle all 3 of these pieces for you so you get the best of both worlds.

To recap, in order to maximize your inbox delivery rates, you simply must have a dedicated IP address / in house email solution. While it may sound overwhelming at first, it's really quite simple once you get it set up.

5 Key Chapter Takeaways

1. Most email service providers use shared IP addresses (if you DO have a dedicated IP with an ESP, then it's important to make sure they're managing the reputation).

2. When you're sending through shared IP addresses, you are only as good as the weakest link.

3. Dedicated IP addresses give you more control over your email program.

4. Consider getting a dedicated IP address on your own server or via an SMTP relay service that understands the complexities of email marketing, like EmailDelivered.com.

5. Be sure you have all the "technical pieces" in place before you start sending out of our own IP.

In the next chapter, we're going to go over the role of content in your messages and the impact that it has on whether or not your messages make it to the inbox.

Mistake #3: Not Testing Message Content

Content is critical when it comes to getting your emails to the inbox (and getting your subscribers to open your messages, click on your links, and take the action(s) that you want them to take).

However, too many people overlook the content and assume it's anything and everything BUT the content in the email message itself.

They think, "I've mailed content like this for years and had no problems. It CAN'T be my content".

It's important to realize that when we refer to email content, we're not simply talking about the words in the email. We're also talking about links, landing pages, and even the from email address that you're using to send your messages from.

This is a BIG mistake because it is the easiest thing to change and the single thing over which you have the MOST control!

The problem is... it takes a bit of planning and testing on your part to ensure optimal results. And most email marketers simply rush to get their emails out and put little thought, preparation or planning into it.

Let's look at a typical scenario that many email marketers face:

It's Tuesday afternoon.

You have to get a promotion out this afternoon (whether it's for a webinar that's scheduled this evening, a promotion that you're sending out this week, or a weekly newsletter).

And you've not even thought about what you're going to write.

You know you've got to get it written, but there are 101 things that are grabbing your attention. A call comes in... You have to answer some customer support tickets... You're working on a new sales funnel that's supposed to go live TOMORROW... Or anything else that takes your attention from writing that email that's got to get out (even though the email is going to generate revenue directly!).

So, when the time finally comes to write the email, you're in a rush because now you're under the gun with a deadline. You're not really feeling all that creative and you certainly don't have any time to "test". So you hammer something out quickly and sent it out in a rush. Who really has time to test anyways, right?

Who has time to check blacklists and content filters on top of it all?

The answer SHOULD BE: **YOU!**

The consequences of NOT doing things are too big not to! Testing is as important as sending the message itself!

Again, one of the primary factors when it comes to getting your emails to the inbox is CONTENT. It's not enough to simply "mask" trigger words or change out a word here and there.

Most "spam filter services" are simply checking against databases that look at specific words in the email (like "drug", "free", "rich", etc.). Too many of these individual words may cause a high spam score. However, these are not necessarily the same things that ISPs look at when determining whether your message passes the spam test or not!

NOTE: It's generally a good idea to use this as a first line of defense and make sure you're not using too many of the keywords the spam checker in your email client detects. We recommend a score of <1 if you're using a built in spam checker based on Spam Assassin or a similar tool.

Keep in mind, however, the ISPs are FAR more sophisticated.

Another problem with looking solely at individual words or phrases is that a lot of marketers will try to mask these words by changing "free" to F.R.E.e or "money" to muney. There are a few problems with this line of thinking:

1. You hurt your credibility with your subscribers. Your subscribers either sense that you're trying to be sneaky OR they think that you're just plain sloppy.

2. If your email makes it to an email administrator, you most certainly look like a spammer!

In other words, let's say that your emails get blocked for some reason and it requires an email administrator to intervene.

These are the guys on the OTHER side that are determining whether or not to let your emails through. Imagine being in their shoes...

They get an email from someone requesting that their emails not go to the spam folder or that a block is removed. They review the message and find a lot of words disguised in order to hide certain words! Naturally they think, "if they're sending legitimate email, why would they be trying to use tricks? It looks like spam and smells like spam, so I'm going to mark it as spam!"

3. It doesn't work as you might expect! This had more of an impact a decade ago, but the ISPs (the Gmails, Hotmails, Yahoos, and AOLs of the world) are FAR more sophisticated with their filtering algorithms. Now, that doesn't mean you shouldn't take these words into account and modify accordingly. If someone is using an email address protected by a service such as spam assassin, for example, these individual words still may cause some problems with your mail.

NOTE: just because your internal spam checker says the content is not spam does NOT mean the ISPs will agree.

Here are a few things to pay attention to with your content:

1. Check Against Spam Filters as A Baseline Test

While I did mention that an individual word here or there is not likely going to destine your email to the spam folder, it is still worth paying attention to and changing the word or phrase to another that is not picked up with the filters. We recommend that you keep that spam filter score as close to 0 as possible.

But wait! You just said individual keywords aren't necessarily a problem

That's correct! In and of themselves, single words are not generally going to a cause a problem with your email. BUT... there is a caveat, the combination of words and use of multiple words in the context of the entire email can cause problems.

The general rule of thumb is that if "SpamAssassin" thinks your email is "spam", there's a good chance that the more sophisticated ISP filters will categorize the message as spam. Conversely, just because Spam Assassin DOESN'T pick up keywords/keyword phrases, doesn't mean that the ISPs won't pick up on the overall message content, context, topic, etc.

2. Watch Links In Your Email Messages

The actual links in your messages could be causing you trouble with your inbox placement. This includes the "from" address, the sending domain, link trackers, and even landing pages. If any of these has a bad reputation or is on a blacklist such as Barracuda or URIBL, then you can see an increase in messages going to the spam folder.

We covered these a bit in Chapter 1, but it's worth mentioning again here as they relate to content, in particular.

From address

This is the domain you are using in the "from" field in your email software. This may be "support@YOURDOMAIN.com". In this case, the "from" address is YOURDOMAIN.com. If that domain has any problems with its reputation, then you run the risk of having all of the emails from that address, regardless of your provider, go to the spam folder.

Sending domain

Generally, this is going to show up in the return-path part of your message headers.

We recommend having total control over your email program. This means sending from your own domain. For example, you may be hosting an email software on your server and sending from there. That's the domain that we're referring to. If you're using an email service provider, then you're stuck with the sending domain that they use for all of their customers.

Links in the body

The links in your email message could also be causing you problems. It used to be as simple as changing a link to a tracking link. However, most of the ISPs see right past that. So, it's important to pay attention to the link displayed AND the landing page (where the subscriber actually arrives once they've clicked the link).

NOTE: This includes links to images in your messages as well!

3. NUMBER of links in your messages

I was troubleshooting for someone a few weeks back and they were trying to figure out why they were going to the spam folders...

They had 18 (yes, EIGHTEEN) links going to the offer. This falls under the "looks and feels like spam to the ISPs." This is almost, if not equally, as bad as the one liner emails that say "To find out the secret to [fill in the blank], click here" with nothing else in the email message!

It comes down to some common sense! Generally, you only need a couple of links in your email for the call to action. The most we ever include, even in long emails, is 4, and that's for an email that's got a number of paragraphs in it.

4.   Overall content.

I had a prospect contact me a short while ago to ask what we could do to help him get out of the spam folder.

After reading his content, it was clear that nobody could really help him with his existing content. He needs to rework the messaging in order to fix his problem. PERIOD.

TIP: Also pay attention to your footers and disclaimers. You may find that the content being used in this section of your email is causing your mail to be filtered. We've seen this on a number of occasions in many different markets, including real estate, stocks, investing, health and fitness, survival, and biz opp. to name a few, and they are becoming more and more of a problem when it comes to content filtering.

5.   HTML content and formatting

Just as your webpages show up differently in different browsers, your HTML emails show up differently in different clients.

If there are any code errors that the ISPs don't want to see, you'll get dinged on that too. There are lots of resources for testing HTML formatting for email such as EmailOnAcid.com, for example.

How to Get Your Content to Pass the Spam Test

Here's a simple "content" checklist to ensure that your content is up to par and not causing any substantial issues that are causing your emails to end up in the junk folder.

1. Check your content against a spam filter. While a single word here and there isn't going to necessarily put you in the spam folder, too many of these words and certain combinations can cause some problems. Try to get your score as close to zero as possible!

2. Test all of the links in your email against services like URIBL or Barracuda to ensure they aren't on any blacklists.

3. Limit the number of call to action links to a max of one for every 100 - 150 words.

4. Let someone else read your email before you send it out and score it. On a scale of 1-10, how "spammy" is this message? Is the call to action clear? Etc.

5. Check your HTML formatting using a service like Litmus.com or EmailOnAcid.com (free trial).

TIP: Use the free trial to develop a template with proper formatting and use that for all future email messages.

6. TEST! The best thing to do is send yourself a test message in each of the major email services and massage the content until it gets to the inbox. Keep in mind, that different ISPs also weight the quality of

"mailboxes" as well as the data going into it (so it's best to use mailboxes that are actually actively being used)!

To recap...

Content is one of the elements over which you have control regardless of what service you are using for your email. It's up to you to test your content and to ensure that you are paying attention to the components over which you have control.

5 Key Chapter Takeaways

1. Content is one of the key reasons that email messages wind up in the spam folder, and it's the single easiest component that you can control, regardless of your email service provider.

2. Don't try to be sneaky with buzzwords like free or money. A single word or phrase is not likely to cause your message to get sent to spam.

3. Always test your messages in each of the email clients before sending (and edit the content, if necessary, until the message inboxes)

4. Check the domains in your emails against blacklists to ensure that the tracking domains as well as the landing domains do not have a poor reputation.

5. Verify your HTML formatting is correct using a service like Litmus.com or EmailOnAcid.com

In the next chapter, we're going to cover what you need to know about "complaints". We'll talk about what complaints are, how to use them to improve your email program, and how to reduce the number of complaints your emails generate.

Mistake #4: Not addressing high complaint rates

The issue of complaints is a hot topic. It is one that can cause your account to be instantly terminated if you're using an established ESP.

If you're using your OWN infrastructure, it can cause you some significant reputation problems which translate into long term deliverability problems. In some cases, the only solution is to scrap your program and start from scratch.

NOTE: This is NEVER the recommended solution and should be done ONLY in the event that all other options have been exhausted.

What is a "Complaint"

Let's quickly define what a "spam complaint" is.

A spam complaint is simply when one of your subscribers reports your email message as spam to their ISP, such as Yahoo, Hotmail, AOL, etc. Every time someone does this, it has a negative impact on your reputation.

Let's take a sidestep here because this is a common comment that comes up when we talk about "spam complaints"

The first thing most people say is: *"But wait! Everyone on my list has "opted in" to receive my emails. It's not spam!"*

Lots of people think that "spam" is just the Viagra ads or the emails from Nigeria asking you to wire bunches of money!

Other people think that spam is simply any mailing that violates the "Can-Spam" law.

The assertion that you are not sending "unsolicited" email would be correct. However, you may STILL be sending "UNWANTED" email! And that is the big difference.

Some of the common reasons people complain (i.e. mark your email messages as spam), assuming you have good list building practices, include:

- They don't recognize you as the sender (i.e. You instantly change who the messages are coming from and they don't recognize the name).

- They forgot they signed up (too little frequency in your messaging).

- You send TOO MANY emails! (too MUCH frequency in your messaging).

- The information you're sending to them is no longer relevant.

- Your unsubscribe process is not simple! (Hidden unsubscribe link or an unsubscribe link that takes them to a page where they have to re-enter their details, for example)

The acceptable level for complaints varies, but is generally quite low (less than .01%). That means roughly 1 complaint per thousand messages sent is the max you'll want to hit. The larger your list, the lower that percentage should be.

Most people think that a complaint is an isolated incident. In other words, if Mary Jane clicks the spam button, Mary Jane just won't get your email messages anymore.

And while that is true to a degree... if you get more than a handful of these, then it can begin to impact your overall reputation and send most, if not all, of your email to the spam folder for a given ISP.

In other words, the ISPs say, "You know what? Marketer Bob gets a decent number of complaints. It seems that people don't like his emails too much. To provide a better customer experience, we better send all their email messages to the spam folder".

So, while one or two may affect only the individual subscriber(s), too many begins to affect your overall program.

High spam complaints indicate a few potential problems with your email program.

These include:

1. Lack of consistency

If your communication with your list is sporadic, subscribers "forget" that they signed up for your email list and, as a result, are more likely to hit the spam button, simply because they don't recognize you or don't remember signing up.

Fix: Get a consistent mailing schedule. At a minimum you should be sending out a weekly e-zine or newsletter that provides value. This way, your subscribers will be used to hearing from you on a regular basis.

2. Too much email

You are simply emailing your list TOO much. They just don't want to get 3 emails a day from you! (or 3 emails a week, depending on your list and your the expectations you've set up from the beginning).

Keep in mind that there is no right or wrong number of emails to send in a given period of time. It's based on the expectations that your subscribers have and whether or not you are meeting those expectations.

Fix: Offer a downsell option. Maybe they want to receive a weekly newsletter or product updates, but they don't want to be sold another product or service 7 days a week, twice per day!

3. Message mismatch

The emails you're sending are not what the subscribers expect - or want - to receive from you. For example, when we were marketing to our real estate subscribers, we did a special promotion to the entire list regarding an Internet Marketing course. It wasn't a good fit, and they let us know by clicking the spam button!

It didn't matter that it made logical sense to us that they would want to know how to market their real estate business online and/or generate an additional stream of income.

Fix: Pay VERY close attention to your complaints and watch to see which messages generate the highest complaints. Evaluate those messages and try to determine why they didn't like those campaigns. If you have a segment of your list that IS interested, send future offers to that segment ONLY. (See Chapter 5)

NOTE: For maximum success in this day and age, it comes down to sending the "right message, at the right time, with the right frequency".

Subscribers that are no longer engaged, are receiving the wrong type of messaging, and do not receive messages at the desired frequency are the most likely to hit the "spam" button!

4. Prior deliverability issues.

This happens QUITE frequently when we bring on new customers. They come over after they've had a delivery issue with another email service provider, and once everything is set up properly, their emails start hitting the inbox. That's great except that people forgot all about them since their emails hadn't been coming to the inbox for week, months, even years in some cases.

There's a strategy for working through this, but if you're using a new service, understand that this is not uncommon. And it could just be a temporary issue.

Fix: Follow a thorough warm up schedule with a provider than understands your situation and how to work through it properly.

How to Reduce Your Spam Complaints

Here are 10 simple things that you can do to reduce your spam complaints.

1. Manage your feedback loops.

Any time someone clicks the "spam" button in your email client, they should be removed from your list immediately. We recommend putting them on the suppression list (i.e. the do not contact list). If you're using an ESP, this will be automatic.

2. Be clear with expectations.

What are people opting in for and how often are they going to get emails from you. Just because they purchased Product A, doesn't mean that they have given you permission to email them 5 times a day with other offers.

3. Use your "From Address", "Subject Line", and "Preview Pane" as branding elements.

For example, use the same from email address/domain name every time you send and ask new subscribers to proactively whitelist you and use something like "[EMD] Subject Line". This makes sure, at the very least, that they recognize you.

4. Make the OPT OUT process EASY!

Don't hide your unsubscribe text in 2pt font at the bottom of your message, require subscribers to re-enter their email address after they've clicked the link, etc. KEEP IT SIMPLE! (Otherwise, they're going to hit the "spam" button because it's just easier).

5. Monitor the "reply-to" email address.

In other words, don't use a do-not-reply@yourdomain.com! You want people to be able to request to unsubscribe by simply sending a reply email.

6. Test Frequency of Emails.

If you send too many emails, you may overdo it. If you don't send enough, they won't remember who you are. (Remember, everyone is inundated with information these days and out of sight = out of mind!)

7. Offer a "Manage Subscriptions" page where people can downgrade their subscriptions.

Instead of your daily email, let them choose to get only your once/week digest. This will decrease spam complaints AND keep people on your list that would have otherwise unsubscribed for good. Be sure to name your lists so that subscribers know what the different lists are so that they are clear as to which lists they want to stay subscribed to.

8. Include a 1-click unsubscribe in all of your emails.

If people have to take too many steps to get off of your list, they're much more likely to hit the "spam" button, which increases your complaint rate and lowers your overall reputation, and consequently your deliverability. NEVER require subscribers to re-enter his/her email address or go through excessive confirmation screens. If someone wants off of your list, make it easy.

BONUS TIP: You can always market to them via Facebook to try to win them back.

9. Test your unsubscribe process regularly.

Keep an eye on your complaints. If you're getting higher than normal complaints, then you'll want to take a look at your unsubscribe process and make modifications accordingly.

10. Include an anchor text link that says "report as spam" that is a one click unsubscribe. For people that are angry, they may choose that link, thinking they are "reporting" you rather than go through the ISP. This is simply an unsubscribe rather than a complaint against you.

NOTE: This will only work in the HTML versions of your messages.

The bottom line is that complaints and your unsubscribe process often go hand in hand. Use common sense when it comes to the "unsubscribe". Let people get off of your list easily and quickly and you'll reduce your complaints. Pay attention to the complaints you DO receive and optimize your email program to minimize the complaints you're getting and, consequently, increase subscriber interaction and value per subscriber.

Now that we've covered complaints and unsubscribe Dos and Don'ts in detail, let's move on to Mistake #4: Doing the Same Thing Over & Over... (and Expecting Different Results)

To recap, complaints are a general indicator of an email campaign or, possibly, a problem with your entire email program. You should strive to keep complaint rates as low as possible and evaluate when and why you're getting complaints in order to make necessary changes to correct any issues.

5 Key Chapter Takeaways

1. Complaints occur when subscribers hit the spam button instead of unsubscribing naturally from your list.

2. Too many spam complaints can cause your ESP to shut you down OR cause deliverability problems (if you're using a dedicated solution).

3. High spam complaints can indicate a few potential issues including (1) lack of consistency, (2) too much email, (3) the wrong type(s) of messages, or (4) an indicator your previous ESP was not getting emails delivered to the inbox.

4. Make it easy for people to unsubscribe. Do not require extra steps or hoops for them to jump through.

5. Use your complaints to identify problems and improve your email program.

In the next chapter, you're going to learn how to increase open rates and click through rates.

Mistake #5: Doing the Same Thing Over & Over and Expecting Different Results (Not Running Re-Engagement Campaigns or Segmenting Your Subscribers)

Have you ever found yourself doing the same thing over and over and over, but expecting different results?

In other words, are you still marketing via email the same way that you were a year ago, or even five or ten years ago? A large majority of email marketers are!

You see... in the earlier days of email marketing, we didn't have nearly as much sophistication at our fingertips. It was kind of a big deal to be able to address each subscriber individually! Add in a few merge fields and we were all advanced email marketers.

Too many people are still stuck back in 2009 when it comes to email marketing (even if they just started marketing last week!).

And yet they wonder why they are seeing a drop in open rates, click through rates, and overall profits with their email marketing. They've been marketing to the same subscribers the same way for too long, without looking at each subscriber as an individual and targeting messages to the individuals at the other end of the message.

In other words, they assume that EVERYONE on their list wants to receive:

- Weekly webinar/teleseminar invites

- Affiliate offers and promotions

- New product notification

- Weekly newsletter

- Solo promotions for other marketers

- [Fill in any type of email marketing you engage in here]

Or they have the attitude "They're on my list and so they get everything, like it or not!"

The problem with this is that you have people on your list with varying levels of interests and/or communication preferences. So it only makes sense that people become less engaged the more you send them emails that aren't in line with their interests.

The answer most marketers have for this is to just email MORE frequently!

I actually saw a thread not too long ago in a private message group to which I belong. One guy said, "I'm not getting the same kinds of opens I was getting before. It's the same list and the same offers. I'm not sure what the problem is."

The next response was, "Dude... the answer is SIMPLE. Just email them more. Send 3 in a day instead of one and you'll make more money!"

YIKES!

Your subscribers start tuning out your emails. Your messages just become "noise" in their inbox. They may choose to unsubscribe or, worse, tell their ISP that your emails are spam by clicking the "Report As Spam" button in their email client. (See Mistake #4 for more on Complaints).

This is critical because in addition to your subscriber's activity, or lack thereof, ISPs are looking at engagement rates as a factor for determining inbox placement, so if 99% of your subscribers are not engaged, the ISPs may ultimately decide that all of your emails are spam, so that 1% doesn't even get your messages anymore.

So, the question then begs... "Why do people continue to do this?"

There are a number of reasons:

1. They don't know better;

2. They don't know HOW to do anything different;

3. Their email software doesn't allow them to do anything different (or at least how to do it easily);

4. Lazy!

I'm going to assume that you fall under reasons 1 through 3 ;-), so let's go ahead and talk about some things that you can do, why you should do them, and how!

Improving Engagement

There are a number of things you can do to improve your subscriber engagement.

Segment Your List

First off, you should NOT be sending the same emails to every subscriber on your list. Even if you're emailing out an invitation to a webinar, you should consider sending out several versions of the email to different segments on your list, appealing to their specific interests.

So what types of things can you segment?

This will depend largely on your list, your audience, the type of data you can/do collect, and so on. You can segment based on criteria such as:

- Male / Female (if it relates to your audience)

- Products Purchased

- Lists Subscribed to (look at combinations to see what their overall interests are)

- Webinars/Teleseminars registered for/attended

- People that have opened a campaign

- People that have NOT opened a campaign

- Subscribers that haven't opened any emails in X period of time

- How long they've been on your list

- Customers vs prospects

- Interests (assuming you have a way to collect this data)

- Etc. (Fill in anything that is related to your market that you could potentially collect data on).

You might be saying, "But wait! I was always told to ask for the minimum to get the optin".

There are a few schools of thought on this, and this isn't the place to cover lead capture theories... HOWEVER, you can absolutely use surveys and other types of lead capture campaigns to gather more data from your subscribers. You can do this as a second step in the optin process in the future, during a promotion, etc.

But you'll notice from the list above, that there are quite a few criteria that you can use for segmenting purposes that are behavior-based and not user defined. It just takes a bit of planning and organization. In other words, you don't have to ASK them if they've purchased a product or to which lists they're subscribed. But you would need to ask them for interests or concerns.

For example, when we offer email deliverability assessments, the first step in the cycle is to get their basic information: Name, email address, and optin page (so we can do a basic assessment).

Then, if they choose to have a more thorough assessment, we ask them more questions so we can get a better handle on what it is the real pain points are. These include:

- Who is your current email provider?

- How big is your list?

- How often to you send email?

- What is your biggest challenge with email right now?

- Etc.

This allows us to get more information so that we can better serve the subscriber. Plus it provides us more information as to what services they are most likely in need of and/or interested in.

Run Re-Engagment Campaigns

If people aren't opening your messages, there's no reason to continue to email them over and over again. I know the theory is that "they could open an email SOME DAY when circumstances change." But for most markets, this is really the exception, not the rule.

As a result, you should run re-engagement campaigns every 90 days at a minimum.

What is a re-engagement campaign?

A re-engagement campaign is nothing more than going back and trying to get people that haven't opened your emails in several months to start opening your emails again. In order for this to work, you'll need to put some thought into the campaigns and come up with a new approach.

After all, the emails they've BEEN getting aren't interesting them enough to open, so you'll need to do something different. Something that will catch their attention.

This means a brand new approach to your subject lines.

It may mean even changing the "from" name to something that stands out a bit more or grabs their attention.

The whole purpose of a re-engagement campaign is to get them to raise their hand and say "Yes, I do still have a pulse and I AM still interested in your emails".

If they're not, get rid of them... Or better yet, upload them to Facebook and run a targeted ad campaign to bring them back, but emailing them over and over again with no response is not doing you any good, and it's certainly not improving their user experience.

Remove Un-Engaged Users (or At Least Downgrade Them)

Too many people are obsessed with list size rather than list quality. I suspect this has to do with email swaps, JVs, and affiliate offers, but it's really kind of a useless metric. What you really want to know is how many people OPEN emails rather than how big the list is. (More on list building and email list size when we talk about Mistake #8).

You really do want to remove unengaged users every 60-90 days (or at least downgrade them to a lesser frequency). I know this goes against what a lot of people think (and lots of marketers simply don't want to reduce the numbers of subscribers on their list).

BUT... as I mentioned before, this is NOT helping you and it is likely hurting you. As ISPs see less engagement, they're MORE likely to send more of your messages to the spam folder.

Here are a few ways to handle unengaged users assuming that you have run a re-engagement campaign to capture anyone that had not been opening your emails recently. We'll look at these using a "good", "better", "best" approach.

"Good" - Send less frequently. For example, consider just a weekly or monthly newsletter out to these subscribers. Or if they're all customers, send only product updates for the products they've purchased.

"Better" - Email the less engaged (unengaged) subscribers through another service, different "from" address, etc. If you're using a dedicated email solution, which we do recommend, this is even more important to keep the reputation separate.

"Best" - Remove these people from your list. It doesn't matter if you have 2,000,000 people on your list if only 10,000 are actually interested in what you have to say. It's better to have 10,000 high quality subscribers over 2 million 'dead' names! Consider using other methods to bring them back. For example, upload the people that are no longer opening your emails to Facebook and try to re-engage them there and entice them to come back to your list.

Let Subscribers Manage Their Own Preferences

Always let subscribers manage their preferences. Instead of a simple "one click unsubscribe," offer them the option to downgrade or opt out of multiple lists.

For example... let's say you have a weekly webinar series, a content newsletter, and a special promotions list. You would simply include a link at the bottom of your email next to your one click unsubscribe that says "Manage Subscription" or "Update Subscriptions".

Once they click on the link, they should have the option to update their email address and opt to change the frequency of email from you. For instance, let them choose to stay on the weekly newsletter or to receive a Friday recap of all the emails that were sent out during the week, but get off of the daily email promotion. (Think Google Groups preferences, if you're familiar with the options there).

You might be thinking, "If they don't want the daily offers, they can unsubscribe. They're gonna get what I send them. It's the cost of being on my list!" Just keep in mind, they're going to unsubscribe and/or complain. It's always better to have a subscriber that WANTS to get your emails on a lesser frequency than to lose them altogether. PLUS, you can still put offers in your newsletter and invite them back into different funnels that way.

To recap, it's no longer enough to just blast your emails out to your entire list and to hope for the best results. ISPs have gotten more sophisticated. Subscribers have gotten more sophisticated. And the technology has gotten more sophisticated. As a result, it's critical that you up your email game!

1. Segment your list. If you've not already been segmenting, it's never too late to start. Create some surveys to collect data that you can use in your marketing in exchange for a special bonus gift.

2. Gather as much information about your subscribers as possible over time (including subscriber-stated preferences AND behaviors.)

3. Run re-engagements regularly to clean out the dead weight.

4. Remove unengaged subscribers between 90 - 180 days at the most. Consider starting a re-engagement strategy between 60-90 days or dropping frequency.

5. Let subscribers manage their own preferences.

In the next chapter, we're going to discuss the biggest mistakes with email affiliate marketing.

Mistake #6: Using Affiliate Swipe Copy "As-Is"

If you've done any kind of affiliate marketing, chances are you're probably guilty of simply copying and pasting the swipe copy into your email client and hitting the send button.

I get it. We're all busy and that's the whole point of swipe copy, right?

Affiliate managers provide it for lazy marketers!

While this also can impact the product owner, we're going to focus on how it impacts the "affiliate," the person sending the offer out to his/her list.

The impact can be significant. In fact, we've had clients come over to EmailDelivered because they've gotten SHUT OFF for simply promoting someone else's offer and using the copy provided to them.

In other words, their email service provider LITERALLY shut off their account because of the offer that they mailed out. Now I know that sounds unfair, but the ESP can certainly enforce their own rules as they see fit.

While that is an extreme example of what can happen, other more common problems include:

- All of your promotions for this campaign wind up in the spam folder (In which case, you don't make money from the promotion because your subscribers aren't getting the emails).

- Your domain and/or IP develops a bad reputation, which results in longer term deliverability problems.

- You lose valid subscribers due to multiple soft bounces. In other words, the messages get blocked before they even get to the spam folder. This is what we call a bounce and with many ESPs, if you get 3 of these types of bounces, the subscribers that bounced are automatically removed from your list.

Ultimately, the person hitting the send button in their email client (that's you!) is responsible for how the promotion performs to his/her list and what happens on the other side of that.

It's your job as the list owner to determine which promotions are going to appeal to your list - even if that means not participating in a big launch. It's also your job to determine the best way to introduce the product or service to the list and how to promote. Often the swipe copy makes sense for the lists belonging to the product creator, but not to yours... It's also not written in your tone or taking advantage of the unique relationship YOU have with your own list.

So let's cover different types of affiliate promotions because they will each have a different impact on you.

1. Personalized Endorsement

A personalized endorsement is an email from you to your list promoting a product or service that you TRULY endorse. For this type of offer, we'll assume that you have personally used the product or service and can speak from your own experience. In a case like this, you've probably got a pretty good idea of what you'd like to say and how this will benefit your list.

As a result, you don't need to use general affiliate swipe copy. These types of promotions will almost ALWAYS out perform any other type of affiliate offer, assuming that you have a relationship with your list, that they are connected to YOU (and that they give weight to things that you recommend).

Certainly, you can use swipe copy as a guideline to make sure you hit on some of the key points, but it's best to include your own endorsement, your personal story with the product or service and your heart felt testimonial.

Generally, these types of emails will have little adverse impact on deliverability because you're not simply copying and pasting an email that 100 other people are all mailing out at the same time on the same day.

You're actually writing a real email to your audience.

ANY time that you can do these types of affiliate promotions, you'll see better results than with other types of affiliate promotions.

Engagement (opens, clicks, and actual conversions) will typically be much higher with these kinds of offers as well, assuming the sales sequence for the product owner converts. Complaints will also be much lower because you are adding value and your unique perspective...

NOTE: As we mentioned in Mistake #3: Content Is King, you will want to keep in mind the basic content principles we discussed such as checking landing page URLs against blacklists such as URIBL, for example prior to sending.

NOTE: There is one potential caveat here and that is if you are promoting a product or service that is available on an affiliate network. See #3 below.

2. Industry-Wide Product Launches

Lots of marketers participate in these and they can be a huge source of income. However, if you're not careful, they can also create a huge problem for your email marketing program including deliverability, inbox placement, blacklisting, overall reputation, and even getting kicked off of your email provider in extreme cases.

Why do these types of promotions cause so many more problems than a personal endorsement?

Well first and foremost, launch URLs are FAR more likely to wind up on blacklists, so you'll absolutely want to check the URLs prior to sending out your campaigns EVEN IF you have a tracking link in front of it. Remember, ISPs are smart enough to see past the link in the message.

How to Participate In Product Launches Without Negative Impact

1. Ask to place the sales video on your own website.

If you have a relationship with the product owner, see if you can place the sales video or sales copy on your own website. Include your "bonus package" under the video and ask that the link goes directly to the order form, rather than the sales page.

TIP: If you are running a product launch, consider these things for your affiliates and get creative. Remember, one or two bad affiliates can hurt the launch for you and all of your affiliates.

In many cases, this is not possible. The product owner is just too busy and doesn't want to have to manage a bunch of affiliates with their content all over the web.

2. Use a "presell" page to frame the reader.

When it is NOT possible to have the sales video on your own site, consider a "presell" page to frame the reader with a personal video explaining what they are about to see and why they should buy from you. Most people on your list know the drill now! They realize that if they buy from you, there's gonna be a massive bonus pack exclusive to you!

So... instead of highlighting the bonuses in the email only, consider sending them to a page on your own website first to frame them.

Then, use the affiliate link on a button on your own page to send them to the sales page for the actual product.

Both of these options will also you to eliminate any problems with the URL since you won't be sending to the actual landing page directly from your email.

NOTE: Even if you have your own tracking link that goes to the affiliate tracking URL, and THEN to the landing page, the ISPs can see the destination URL and this absolutely can impact your deliverability.

3. Change the swipe copy.

If you remember for the chapter on content, it's not ONLY the URL, it's also the message content that's important for deliverability

In cases of launches, there are often dozens (in some cases 100s+) of people sending out the very same promotion. Most people will leave the affiliate copy as is. MAYBE they'll add in their bonus pack, but the bulk of the copy will be the same across all of the affiliates.

The problem with this is that as people start to see these messages over and over again, they start to click the spam button. The ISPs then look at the content and determine the swipe copy is spam and drop the messages in the junk folder, even IF YOUR subscribers aren't complaining about YOU. The fact that the content appears spammy and has triggered complaints from OTHER senders is going to impact you.

For instance, if you look in your spam folder in Gmail, you'll often see messages like this:

Why is this message in Spam? It's similar to messages that were detected by our spam filters.

This generally happens because the message content is either identical to other messages that have caused complaints or is reasonably similar.

The bottom line is this: If it's worth promoting, it's worth taking a few minutes and writing *your own emails* using only the key points from the product owners swipe file to, again, make it your own. You will see higher inbox placement, higher open rates, and lower complaints when you do because you're not getting lost in the spam folder OR making your subscribers mad, all of which ultimately hurt your reputation.

#3. Affiliate Networks

While I typically do not advocate these, I realize that they are a part of many of our clients' businesses and there are folks that use these networks for merchant processing, so it is important to address these types of offers and promotions.

First and foremost, be VERY careful with the links. Many affiliate network URLs are pretty much blacklisted by the major ISPs. So the URLs, even if they are redirects, can cause problems with your content, causing your messages to head straight to the spam folder. While the domain won't show up on traditional blacklists, the ISPs maintain their own algorithms and know which websites account for a good bit of spam traffic, many of these are affiliate and CPA networks.

In addition, these types of offers also generate the highest number of complaints. If you're using an ESP, this can get you a stern warning and/or shut off completely. More than twenty percent of our clients come over because they've hit a complaint threshold with a strict email service provider, often because of these types of promotions.

Depending on your market, these types of offers can also hurt your reputation with your list. People are pretty quick to catch on when they're just being treated like a cash machine and getting sent offer after offer, with no real value.

So if you ARE going to promote these products, first make ABSOLUTELY certain that the products are a great fit for your list and a match for your market. I would actually recommend that you purchase the product, go through the sales funnel and go through the product. If you're going to recommend it to your list, it seems a small price to pay! And most of these types of offers are pretty inexpensive.

Then, use the strategies discussed in #1 and #2 in this chapter to help with the emails, links, and so on. Your results will be better overall. You'll sell more products and produce fewer complaints. Simply sending an email with a couple of sentences and "click here to buy now" is not going to do you or your email program any good in the long run.

To recap, when it comes to affiliate promotions of any kind, there are 3 CRITICAL things to consider:

1. Links - You should ABSOLUTELY check all links against spam filters and blacklists. Even if the URL is clean, you may want to consider a landing page on your own site in the middle as a presell page to frame the reader.

2. Swipe Copy - Don't be lazy! Write your OWN copy whether it's a one on one endorsement or a product launch promotion in which you are participating.

3. Watch out for affiliate networks - They've gotten a bad rap over the years for good reasons. It's an easy target for spammers to make a quick shot of cash. If you're going to use these networks, be sure to use your own copy, use intermediary landing pages, and evaluate the product prior to promoting it.

1. Using affiliate swipe copy "as is" can not only cause your promotional emails to wind up in the spam folder, but can also impact your long term email deliverability.

2. Always use the same voice when communicating with your list (which means you need to rewrite swipe copy in your own voice 100% of the time).

3. Personalized endorsements almost always outperform any other type of affiliate promotion.

4. When participating in product launches, consider using intermediate landing pages to pre-frame/pre-sell the reader.

5. Be very careful when promoting products from affiliate networks.

- In the next chapter, we're going to talk about how to keep your list in tip top shape.

Mistake #7: Email Until They Die or Buy

For one reason or another, too many people are attached to the SIZE of their list and will do just about anything they can to avoid having to remove people from their list. As a result, they live by the philosophy "Email Until They Die or Buy"!

This is a critical mistake because list quality plays a huge role in deliverability and, more importantly, inbox placement.

The bottom line is this: If you continue to send to invalid addresses, full mailboxes, complainers, and non openers, then your reputation will ultimately suffer along with your revenue.

List Hygiene Areas of Opportunity

There are a handful of categories that you need to look at including:

- Bad addresses

- Full mailboxes

- Complainers

- Non openers

Let's talk about why each of these is a problem.

Bad Addresses

A high number of bad addresses is a telltale sign to the ISPs that you simply don't care about list hygiene which tells them that you really don't care about list quality. This is one of the biggest reasons that we see reputation problems. Bad addresses should be quickly identified and immediately removed from your list.

70

If you're using an email service provider or a reputable email software, then there's a good chance the majority of these addresses are automatically removed from your list. However, it's worth verifying this and doing a manual clean up from time to time.

Full mailboxes, in and of themselves, are not necessarily a problem. It's possible that a subscriber has gone on vacation and his/her mailbox has simply filled up for a day or two. While it's not all that common, it's possible and it does happen, especially with business email addresses when people aren't managing quotas.

But... more likely than not, a mailbox fills up when the subscriber has abandoned the mailbox for one reason or another. This is almost always the case when we're talking about the free email service providers. The subscriber decides to set up a new email account. Over time, the mailbox fills up. A little more time goes by and then ISP realizes that the mailbox has been abandoned. The mailbox is then reclaimed and possibly converted to a spam trap. (See Chapter 8 for more information on Spam Traps).

The good news is that the ISPs notify you when a mailbox is full so that you can go ahead and remove the address from your list. Generally speaking, if you get 3-5 "bounces" due to the mailbox being full, you should remove that address from your list. This will ensure that recycled spam traps don't remain in your list and cause damage to your reputation.

Complainers

When someone clicks the "spam" button in their email client, this is a "complaint." When you get beyond the acceptable complaint thresholds, the ISPs may send more of your messages to the spam folder, throttle the rate at which they accept your email, or reject your email entirely. If you're using an ESP, there's a good chance that you'll get a stern warning or, worse, shut off without notice.

NOTE: If you are using an ESP, they will automatically remove the complainers from your list. However, many of them will not provide you with the data to identify the complainers, so if you move services, there's a good chance you'll wind up mailing them again.

Non Openers

The previous 3 categories are pretty self-explanatory and rarely cause a lot of pushback from marketers. However, non openers often generates a bit of a discussion.

Sure, there is always a chance that one of those unengaged subscribers COULD change their mind and buy your product or service at some point in the future. But the percentage of subscribers that do that is so slim that the one or two possible sales at some point in the future simply aren't worth the negative impact.

Over time, if ISPs see that the majority of your subscribers aren't engaging with your messages, they may start to filter more and more of them to the spam folders. This is not necessarily limited to those people that simply aren't engaged. In other words, if 95% of your subscribers aren't opening any of your emails, the ISPs may simply decide that people don't want to get your messages and, consequently, send them all to the spam folder instead of the unique unengaged subscribers, even those 5% that have opened an email from you.

Essentially, all 4 of these categories can cause significant long term delivery problems if not properly handled. Messages may get rejected altogether (aka blocked) or, at best, be sent to the spam folder.

When it comes to bad addresses, full mailboxes and complainers, people generally just don't know there's a problem. When and if they are made aware of the problem, they're quick to fix it.

However, when it comes to non-openers, people simply don't want to part with "possible" buyers on their list. Plus, when people are participating in product launches and affiliate promotions, everyone always wants to know "how big your list is."

When I was in the real estate info business, my list was only about 15,000 people, but I routinely outperformed people that had 10X that on their list. And it's because I had 15,000 active/valid subscribers that I had a relationship with. They opened my emails. They knew that I cared about them and that I wasn't going to put garbage in front of them just to make a buck.

Rather than waiting for subscribers to drop off of your list due to unsubscribing, abandoning an email address, hitting the spam button, and so on, it's best to take a proactive approach to managing your database.

Key Points for List Hygiene

The good news is that list hygiene really isn't that complicated. There are only a few steps to take in order to have a HIGHLY responsive and engaged subscriber base.

1. Follow best practices when it comes to list building.

This will reduce the number of "new" bad addresses that show up in your list (and will virtually eliminate the possibility of spam traps). But even if you have pristine email collection strategies, there's still going to be a certain number of bad addresses over time in your list. People change companies. Websites go out of business. People abandon email addresses, which then fill up and are no longer valid.

TIP: If you're moving email providers, be sure to export only the active subscribers. Many ESPs will let you take ALL of the data, including email addresses that have bounced and been removed from your list. While I'm not suggesting this is malicious, it can harm you when trying to move to a new service. Contact your ESP and ask them to provide you with a copy of your list including the status (i.e. active, bounced, unsubscribed, etc.). You can let them know that you're wanting to create offsite backups to protect your data.

2. Watch your bounces and take action.

Pay careful attention to hard bounces (which are generally bad addresses and should be removed immediately). Remove all other bounces that are not related to a temporary block or issue after 3-5 failed attempts. In other words, if you've tried to mail to a full mailbox 5 times in a row, and the email address has bounced back each time with a code indicating the mailbox is full, remove it. There's a good chance the mailbox has been abandoned. Truth be told, any address that bounces 5 times in a 30 day period should just be removed from your list.

3. Set up Feedback loops with the major ISPs (that have feedback loop programs in place).

This allows you to get a notification any time that someone clicks the spam button so you can remove people from your list (To get a list of current feedback loops, visit: www.emaildelivered.com/feedback-loops).

4. Develop a win-back or re-engagement campaign

Develop a win-back or re-engagement campaign for everyone that hasn't opened an email OR clicked on a link in the past 90 days (this will cover anybody that may not use HTML in their email clients, which is becoming a smaller and smaller number incidentally). If you're not quite ready to go back 90 days, consider going back 6 months for your initial clean up.

Send a 3-5 part campaign ONLY to those subscribers in order to try to re-engage them.

If that fails to work, there are still a few additional options such as uploading them to Facebook and running a targeted campaign to just those subscribers offering them something of value to come back. You may also consider a data append service that can get you phone numbers or mailing addresses for subscribers.

This may cost a few dollars, but depending on the product or service, may well be worth it.

To recap, it's not enough to just continue to mail to your list forever more, regardless of whether or not they are opening your emails. The chance that the subscriber that hasn't opened a message in 2 years is suddenly going to come back and buy from you is so slim that it's not worth the other negative fallout. Just keep a clean list of people that WANT to hear from you.

5 Key Chapter Takeaways

1. Gone are the days where you can just continue to email over and over and over again until the person drops off one way or another.

2. It's important to pay attention to the bounce messages you receive from the ISPs and take regular action.

3. Run frequent re-engagement campaigns to try to recapture people that haven't been "listening" for some time (consider 90 - 180 days to start).

4. Take un-engaged subscribers and run a Facebook targeting campaign to try and offer them something related to the original offer/reason they signed up with you in the first place.

5. Finally, consider running a data append to your list and getting phone numbers and mailing addresses to follow up with different media.

In the next chapter, we're going to discuss buying, renting and trading email lists.

Mistake #8: Buying, Renting, Trading or Scraping Email Addresses

I realize that it can be enticing when you're looking at the prospect of getting 10,000, 100,000 or even 1,000,000+ names for a few dollars (or even for free). It's like an instant business in a box with little to no effort.

But, as the saying goes, nothing in life is free. And, almost always, you're going to wind up on the losing side of the deal.

As long as people have been marketing products and services through email, people have always looked for ways to get more leads and have more prospects to sell to. Obviously, the more people you have on your list, the more money you'll make, right?

Not Exactly!

You see, it's not the size of the list that matters. It's the QUALITY of the list that's important. Certainly, the MORE QUALITY SUBSCRIBERS you can get, that want to hear from you, and are interested in the products and services you are offering, the better!

But, poor list building practices are going to backfire 100% of the time. PERIOD.

This is one area that does not have any shades of gray!

"Bad" List Building Tactics

The "bad" list building tactics that I'm referring to specifically in this chapter include:

Buying Email Lists

This is fairly straightforward. It is enticing when you can purchase a list of 100,000+ names that you can buy for $100. No matter how good they tell you the addresses are, you're going to have a lot of bad addresses, low engagement, and high complaints.

Renting

Rather than purchasing the list, you're renting it for a set number of mailings. The list owner will seed the list with his/her own addresses to ensure that you don't mail to it more times than you've paid for. Instead of "renting," consider doing a media purchase where the list owner mails out on your behalf using your creative.

Trading

Trading lists may seem harmless. After all, there's a good chance that many of the subscribers on your list are on others in your market. They're obviously interested in the topic, so what's the harm. The theory is that everyone shares the same list, but nobody has to spend the money or trade affiliate offers to get the names.

Scraping

List scraping generally uses a "bot" of some sort that scours the web to find email address posted on websites. This is a GREAT way to find a load of spam traps. Most people would never put a valid email address on a website for this reason in particular.

The Negative Impacts...

Here are a few reasons WHY buying, renting, trading or scraping email addresses is a bad idea:

1. Legal Implications:

You're probably familiar with CAN SPAM. If your email program violates the law, you could be subject to a fine of $16,000 PER offense. People that have not signed up to receive emails from you are far more likely to file complaints than those who have, at one point or another, asked for emails from you. You can read the full text of the US CAN SPAM law here: http://www.business.ftc.gov/documents/bus61-can-spam-act-compliance-guide-business

2. Your Email Program May Get Shut Down:

Most ESPs have terms of service that specifically state that you may NOT buy, rent or scrape email addresses. In fact, many will simply not allow you to upload a list of any sort or, if they do allow uploads, they will monitor the quality and if you are getting a lot of complaints or bad addresses, may shut you down immediately.

At the very least, they are likely to refuse the rest of the upload.

If you're using your own dedicated server, there's a good chance your web host will shut you down due to high complaints or bad addresses.

3. Reputation:

Most "purchased" lists also include spam traps and bad addresses, which can be reputation killers! Both of these can get you put on blacklists, causing your deliverability to drop significantly.

NOTE: This is not specific to the IP address. It can also cause problems with your domain. For example, your entire from domain may be blocked (or at least sent to the spam folder) by one or more of the major ISPs.

You may be thinking... "But I have a high quality list. They've verified there are no spam traps and the addresses are valid." Whether this is true or not is another story, but let's say it is for argument's sake.

Even if you DO get your hands on a list that is targeted to your market, is clean of spam traps, and has had the bad addresses removed, these people STILL do not know you. You do not have a relationship with them. And they never asked to receive emails from you. As a result, you are going to have a MUCH higher complaint rate, which can cause (1) your emails to get throttled, (2) your IP address to get blocked, or (3) get you shut down due to high complaints.

Simply changing your IP address in this case will not help. (the past three paragraphs are in font 13 and the rest are 12...did you mean that?)

4. Waste of Resources:

Buying lists not only wastes your money, but it also wastes your time. Regardless of the list quality, the response is going to be low because they don't have a relationship with you and they likely won't recognize you. Consequently, they just won't open the emails.

We have seen people build out extensive promotion sequences to specifically target these types of audiences. And even with a very clear warm up campaign and introductory campaign, it's very hard to generate an ROI on these types of lists. It's ALWAYS better to build a list organically.

5. There Are Better Alternatives to Building a List

At the end of the day, there are lots of other ways to build your list. Some are more expensive than others, of course, but all of them will generate a higher quality list, which in turn, equates to more money in your pocket and a higher return on your investment.

7 List Building Strategies for a Quality List

Building a quality list does not have to be difficult or expensive. Here are 7 strategies that you can use to build, or grow your existing list.

1. Joint Ventures

While you are probably familiar with joint ventures, a list building joint venture may or may not include affiliate sales. In other words, if you have lists similar in size, you may wish to send out a promotion for opt-ins only and each partner keeps his/her leads or sales.

Another spin on this is to pay for opt-ins rather than affiliate sales. (This can be helpful if you're just starting out and don't have a list to which you can cross promote).

NOTE: You can certainly do an affiliate email swap as well and pay one another for the sales. This is just another alternative.

2. Sponsored Emails/Media Buys

There are a number of different ways that you can approach sponsored emails and media buys.

Solo ad - You simply send your creative to a publisher and they mail it out to all, or a portion of, their subscribers. For example, let's say that I have a product that appeals to conservative, white males that listen to talk radio. I may want to test my offer to Glen Beck or Rush Limbaugh by sending out an email to their lists.

In this case, I would send in my creative. They would then approve it (or send it back for a revision), and the email would go out to all, or a segment, of their list.

In line ad - Some advertisers may have sponsored ads within their email newsletters. These can often be much less expensive, but don't have the same results as a solo ad either. You would have a short 1-2 sentence ad with a call to action in their newsletter. Think classified ad in the offline world.

Banner ads - Many sites will also sell ad space on their website or blog that you can rent on a monthly basis

3. Facebook Ads

Facebook is a great way to build your email list, re-engage subscribers who have lost interest, and to create a relationship with a list that you didn't build personally).

If you're building a list from scratch, consider running ads to people that like your competitors pages or fall into your demographic criteria.

If you're using Facebook to re-engage subscribers that are no longer opening your emails (or who have unsubscribed), you'll want to carefully segment those that have lost interest and find out what it was they were interested in when they originally signed up with you and develop a campaign around that particular topic, or product, to bring them back.

This may involve multiple funnels within your Facebook strategy, but will be well worth the effort.

If you've acquired a list of email addresses, upload them to Facebook and run specific campaigns to them in order to capture their attention and bring them into your funnel, where they can opt-in on their own.

4. Other Social Media

Facebook isn't the only social media outlet that offers advertising. Depending on your product or service, and your market, consider looking into both Twitter (https://ads.twitter.com) and LinkedIn (https://www.linkedin.com/ads) for example.

5. Pay Per Click

I won't spend much time here as there are countless books, products, and courses on pay per click advertising. The one thing that I will say here is there's more to PPC than Adwords these days, so look for other alternatives for pay per click advertising that might make sense for you. For example, if you've got great editorial content, check out Outbrain.com.

6. Content Marketing

People use the Internet to find information. The more content that you can provide through multiple channels such as articles, blog posts, press releases, videos, social media, infographics, and so on, the more visitors you will get to your website.

When someone comes to your site after reading quality content from you, they are a much more qualified prospect than someone that comes to you from a straight ad on Google.

This is actually a HUGE part of our inbound marketing strategy and has increased our site visitors tenfold in the past 90 days!

7. Direct Mail

Few people look to direct mail when it comes to building an email list, but when done properly, direct mail can be extremely effective. The best part is that you have little to no competition in this area. Your competitors simply aren't willing to take the time to understand their audience, find lists that contain prospects with similar demographics, or conduct the mailing itself. It's a hidden goldmine that is largely untapped.

Again, I realize that when presented with the opportunity to buy, rent, or even trade a list, it is enticing to say the least. However, very few marketers have any success when taking this approach to list acquisition. More often than not, it causes more problems than opportunities it creates...

To recap, the long and the short of it is, there are lots of ways that you can build a quality list. Ultimately, buying a list is going to cause you more long term issues with deliverability than it's probably worth. As enticing as it may seem to get a few hundred thousand subscribers added to your list for a few dollars, it's important to resist the temptation!

5 Key Chapter Takeaways

 - Buying, renting, or trading email lists (or scraping) is almost always a losing model, regardless of how good your marketing is to try to warm them up.

 - Using "shortcuts" to build your list will damage your email reputation and can potentially impact your deliverability for your current subscribers.

 - Most email service providers and web hosts have strong policies regarding bulk email and list building. Engaging in these strategies may cause your account to be suspended or, worse, terminated without notice.

 - There are lots of valid ways to build a loyal subscriber base that don't have to cost a lot of money.

- Consider using a combination of list building strategies including social media to re-engage unengaged subscribers, recapture unsubscribed leads, and to warm up a cold list.

In the next chapter, we're going to go over how to balance content vs. selling to keep your list happy while making money from every email you send. (When this is done properly, you'll see more sales on every email, including content-heavy messages).

Mistake #9: Not Providing A Balance of Content and Sales Messages

Email Marketing comes down to relationships, plain and simple (we cover this more in chapter 10). And nobody wants a relationship in which they are constantly being SOLD to, no matter how good the product or service may be.

Some people will tell you to never send an email unless you're selling something. After all, the point of being in business is to make money and how can you do that if you don't sell, right?

More on this in a moment!

Then, there's the other side of the coin where people send out nothing BUT content. The theory here is that if they provide nothing but great content 99% of the time, when they DO have something to offer, their subscribers will gobble it up and they'll make loads of money with every offer. This is most common with people just getting started.

Let's take a moment to look at both arguments.

Sell-Sell-Sell

This approach tends to be more prevalent with marketers that have been in the business for a while. There are several scenarios where we see this the most:

They've already exhausted all of their own funnels and content.

They have a more "traditional business" and have a hard time coming up with content.

They've grown bored of their topic.

They've built a business that requires a certain number of sales each month to cover overhead and they're not bringing in a steady stream of new subscribers. Whatever the reason is, it's important to not fall into this trap - EVER!

Let's face it… we're all in business to make money.

In order to make money, you've got to make offers and sell. And while that's true, if your subscribers feel like they are just an automated cash machine, then they're not likely to stick around for too long.

 If you think about the people or companies you engage with most often, there's a good chance they provide some good content, helpful resources, and useful tips for you more often than not.

NOTE: One thing that's important to remember is that not all "selling" is equal.

If you're selling your own products or services in a logical sequence or with special promotions, there's often a bit more tolerance to more frequent offers versus selling one product after the next from affiliate networks. I'm not suggesting affiliate networks are necessarily bad. What I am suggesting, however is that when someone is marketing one after the next and nothing else, it can cause some relationship issues with your list (along with email deliverability problems).

As a member of a number of different networking - and JV - groups, I see this come up over and over again.

It'll be a Monday afternoon and email goes out to the group that says something like this: "I have an opening this week for a promotion. Anybody have a good product that converts?"

Then a bunch of replies come in with people offering their products and pitching their EPC (earnings per click). There's nearly never a mention of what the product is about or mention of the quality of the product.

In and of itself, this doesn't seem harmful. You're part of a network and want to support each other.

Hey, at least you have some sort of relationship with the product owner... It's better than just blindly promoting products from ad networks. So what's the problem?

The problem here is that you're looking at it in terms of "I've got to make money off my list" vs. "How can I provide value to my list" or... "What would be helpful to my list right now?"

Your subscribers will figure this out and stop opening your messages, will unsubscribe from your emails, or, worse, start clicking the spam button in their email client.

The opposite side of this argument is the "Content Only" approach to email marketing.

Content-Content-Content

Often, but not always, this is usually a confidence problem! People are afraid to sell or don't think their offers are going to convert. This tendency is more common with newer Internet marketers, but there are some seasoned marketers that still fall into this trap.

Here's the common argument for this strategy.

"If I provide a TON of really good content for the first few months, then the law of reciprocity will kick in. When I finally decide to sell something, everyone will jump at the offers. They'll feel "obligated" to buy something since I've given them SO much"

NOPE!

They don't feel obligated to open up their wallet, enter their credit card details and buy <u>anything</u>! It's your job to sell it.

The fact is... if you condition people to expect only free content from you, that's the relationship that they're going to expect. They're not just going to buy to reciprocate what you've offered. In fact, you'll get some folks that are plain mad that you tried to sell them anything at all.

Or how about this one...

"I'm going to give them so much value that they're going to say 'Wow, he/she gave me ALL this for free. I can only imagine what I'll get if I pay for it."

NEGATIVE!

In fact, as much as this would make sense, people can only absorb so much information. If you provide too much content, then they don't have to buy. They can implement what you've already given them before they buy. And as we all know, only 3% of people actually implement anything at all. They may INTEND to buy "once they've implemented the free stuff you gave them." The sad reality is that they never implement the first stuff you sent, so they never get around to buying the product.

I know from personal experience that this doesn't work! When I launched my first product back in 2001, I delivered nothing but content for the entire first 30 days. Then, when I tried to "sell" something, my list was NOT happy! They weren't afraid to tell me either ;-)

You need to make money to stay in business, so the content only approach can backfire in a big way and take some time to recover from.

So what can you do about it?

Strike a balance!

Ultimately, there <u>has</u> to be a balance between content and selling. You've got to provide extraordinary value AND make a living. You've got to find a way to keep people opening your emails and manage to sell.

The good news is that it's not rocket science. In fact, it's quite simple really.

There are a couple of proven formulas that you can use. You can even mix and match the different formulas to make sense.

1. Promotion Calendar

I realize that most marketers are scrambling at the last minute to get their emails written and mailed out (I've been guilty as charged more than a time or two myself).

Planning is nice "theory", but is harder to achieve in practice.

BUT... it makes all the difference in the world

Start by planning out the next 2 weeks in advance and build up to a 4-6 month schedule. Keep a few weeks open in the event you have special things pop up that you might need to move things around for. But think of the schedule in terms of a semester course in school. There are certain things that you want to accomplish during that time. This will help you build the offers into a cohesive content plan. Plus, it will really help you provide value throughout the cycle.

You can even let your subscribers know what you'll be focusing on for the next period of time so they can look forward to what's coming.

TIP: Depending on the size of your list and the focus of your brand, you may consider running different calendars for each segment. Think of a college semester with 5 different classes.

Yes, this may sound like a bit more work, but it truly does pay off and once you get it done, you can really put your email promotions on autopilot.

Come up with the calendar and write all the emails in a few days. Then, you've got a few months to focus on other things in your business, like getting traffic, building your list, and working on your marketing funnels.

2. 80/20 Rule (or 70/30)

When you follow this rule, 80% of your email messages will be "content-driven", 20% will be sales-driven. Here's a proven formula for a 7 Day promotion...

Day 1. Send your subscribers really great content, related to the product that you're going to be offering. This is sort of an introduction to the topic itself and gets people salted. You can let them know that you are cooking up something that they'll definitely want to keep an eye out for in a few days.

TIP: If you start the article in the email and finish it on your blog, you'll almost certainly generate additional sales on your blog of other products and services just from the increased traffic.

Day 2. Send another email with some great content. This can be your content or other content such as videos from YouTube, or news stories that help strengthen the conversation about topic X.

TIP: If possible, embed the content on your own website rather than send them to an external site where they can easily get sidetracked.

Day 3. This email should highlight the importance of all the things that you are going to cover in the product you're going to announce tomorrow. This really salts the audience so that they're primed for the offer. They've just had a few days talking about the topic with no promotion whatsoever. You've told them the benefits of whatever it is that your training is going to cover. At this point, your subscribers are already interested in the topic and essentially pre sold on the idea of the product.

Day 4. Announce the product that you're selling/promoting. In this email, you're absolutely pushing the product. You've been talking about the topic for a few days. Let them know what the offer is, why they should take you up on it, what the scarcity is, and so on.

Day 5. Remind them about the offer that you launched on Day 4. Hit the reasons why they need to buy and let them know that there is a limited window (assuming there is a limited time). If not, highlight whatever it is that would entice them to buy right now.

Day 6. Send content again... This content should really talk about all the benefits that they'll receive when they purchase the product. You can mention the offer or the sales page URL in the P.S. or casually in the copy, if done properly. This is best if there is a time limit. If so, you can remind them in the P.S. "By the way, a couple of days ago, I told you about product X. Well, to get {benefit 1}, {benefit 2}, etc., you'll want to pick that up in the next 36 hours before {the price goes up}, {the page comes down}, etc.

Day 7. Final offer for the content. Remind them all of the benefits and bonuses and then include in the P.S. "By the way, if you missed yesterday's email, I covered {the benefits that you covered in your email}. I've included the full article below". It's really good stuff that you'll want to read.

The key to all of this is that on the 5 days that you are providing content, the content needs to be REALLY good content. Then, on the 3 days that you are "selling", you have earned that right! And remember, you can "softly" sell in all of the emails as long as you're subtle about it and the MAIN purpose of the email is to provide content.

NOTICE some of the messages are both sales messages AND content... This is absolutely okay and, in fact, a great way to build value and sell together.

For samples of promotions like the ones discussed in this chapter, visit http://www.EmailMessageWizard.com.

To recap... it's important to strike a balance between content and sales when it comes to communicating with your list. Too much of one, and not enough of the other can hurt your relationship with your list and cause your sales to drop over time.

5 Key Chapter Takeaways

1. Always provide value to your subscribers.

2. Remember that your subscribers are real people and not just a digital cash machine (foster the RELATIONSHIP).

3. Incorporate both selling and content into your email. No sales = no money. No content = no subscribers! Both are equally important.

4. Use a promotional calendar to ensure that you are giving great content and that your overall messaging flows.

5. Balance content and sales into a ratio that works for you, 50/50 at a minimum.

In the next chapter, we're going to cover setting expectations for the relationship and how to meet expectations so your subscribers keep on coming back for more!

Mistake #10: Not Respecting the Relationship

The fact that you made it this far means that you're serious about email marketing and that you generally follow email best practices.

Chances are that you build your list properly and that you're only mailing to people who have given you permission (i.e. opted in through some web form on your website or purchased a product or service from you).

It doesn't matter if they've single opted in or double opted in, the point is that they came to your website, filled out a form, and agreed to receive something from you in exchange for that information.

This is where MOST marketers make a HUGE mistake in thinking that a single optin gives them the right to email at will.

Think for just a moment…

Have you ever opted in to get a freebie such as a free report, or video, or whitepaper only to be bombarded by offer after offer, many of which have little to nothing to do with the reason you originally opted in?

I mean, you TECHNICALLY gave them permission to contact you, right?

Well, yes and no! You gave permission to send you a free ITEM such as a report, an ebook, etc… NOT to add you to their main promotion list to which they send out a morning and afternoon affiliate offer!

This is all too common when it comes to email marketing and it is one of the biggest reasons your subscribers stop paying attention to your messages, choose to unsubscribe, or even click the "spam" button in their email client, causing you not only to have people that are upset with you in your list, but who also are damaging your email reputation and running the risk of getting your email program shut down.

Just because someone opted in to get your "free video" teaching them 'How to Protect Themselves in the Case of A Zombie Outbreak" doesn't mean that they're interested in affiliate offers about "Losing 10 Pounds of Belly Fat." While I'm sure that there are folks out there that can make a "connection" between the two that may even sound legitimate, it still doesn't mean that your subscribers have given you the green light to send them those types of offers.

So what's the big deal, really?

On the surface, it wouldn't seem like this is a big deal. I mean, you're in business to make money and you make money by sending offers to your list.

Sure, some people will stop paying attention or simply unsubscribe... A few people may hit the spam button... So what?

Well, that 'so what?' is where the problem lies.

Let's look at the impact each of these items actions

Each of these plays an important role in your email deliverability, all of which can present a serious problem.

1. Subscribers stop paying attention.

In other words, people stop opening your emails.

They may batch delete all of your messages periodically. I know from personal experience, the first thing I do every morning is do a mass delete of all the junk, which includes any bulk email that I'm no longer interested in.

It takes longer to go and unsubscribe from them all, so I just select a few hundred at a time and hit "delete."

As a result, none of these emails are "opened." The engagement goes WAY down and the ISPs see that people are not opening your emails. They assume that you are not sending content that people are interested in. This is especially true if you're not running reengagement campaigns and removing the deadweight (aka the people that aren't opening your emails at least every 90 days).

When more and more people start tuning out your messages, the ISPs may automatically start filter your messages directly to the junk folder because you just aren't engaging your subscribers. The problem with this is that it generally happens slowly over time so you may not even be aware there's a problem other than you see a slow and steady decline in your metrics.

2. Subscribers opt out.

This is better than clicking the spam button, but it's not a "net positive" in your business. You spend a lot of time and money acquiring subscribers. So why lose them unnecessarily?

Having said that, you WILL have people unsubscribe from virtually every message that you send, but you want to keep that to a minimum. You certainly don't want them to unsubscribe because they feel that you aren't providing any kind of value.

TIP: Pay attention to unsubscribe metrics. This will help you gauge the types of offers your subscribers are resistant to. For example, if you send out a campaign and find a high number of unsubscribes, then you know that those messages aren't resonating with your list and you may want to modify the types of messages you're sending.

3. Subscribers click the spam button.

This is the biggest risk to your email program. When subscribers get frustrated, they're more likely to click the spam button in their email client. When too many subscribers report your messages as spam, there are a number of potential problems that can occur:

- ISPs filter all of your messages to spam

- ISPs rate limit your messages (limit how many messages you can send per hour)

- ISPs block your emails entirely

- Your ESP (email service provider) may shut you down entirely with or without any notice

Trust me... I get the appeal. You're building a list so you want to be able to market offers to it at will. The good news is... there's a right way and a wrong way to do it...

So What's the Solution?

It really comes down to a few things... Here are four things to consider as well as some ideas for ways to increase what you can send to subscribers without the negative implications.

1. Respect Their Permission

Just because they signed up for a single item, doesn't mean that you now have permission to email affiliate offers every day for the next 365+ days. You need to get permission for that. And you need to be up front about what you're going to be sending them right from the beginning.

You can generally send a 10+ day follow up sequence that enhances the offer for which they've signed up. What I'm referring to, specifically, is sending unrelated emails and offers outside of the scope of what they initially subscribed for.

It's important to set the expectations early on, and stick to what you promised. Be up front and clear about what they're going to get and stick to it!

This is a brand new relationship and you need to think about it like that.

Imagine you're meeting for a first date at a coffee shop. That's it... You don't have permission to call twice a day every day. You've got to have a successful first date at the coffee shop. If that goes well, then perhaps you go to dinner and then a movie, and so on.

Build the relationship and get permission for additional contact along the way. If you're providing value, this is not very difficult!

2. Allow Subscribers to Move Through Your Sequences & Funnels

I would recommend ALWAYS running an autoresponder sequence of a minimum of 7-10 days to help them consume the initial optin item, build a relationship and invite them to sign up for a regular newsletter, other products/interests, and so on. This way, you're adding value by helping them consume the item AND you're opening the door for other types of communication.

As long as you've gotten the permission up front, then they're not likely going to get upset with you.

The question generally comes up AFTER the initial sequence has run out. You want to make sure that you're not bombarding them with unrelated emails and offers. If you want to push them into another funnel, then you'll want to get permission or at least some gauge of interest from them and send them the sequences they're most interested in.

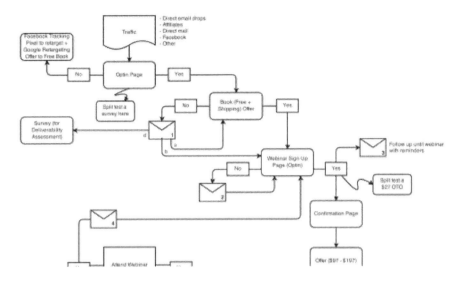

NOTE: You don't need to require them to opt in each and every time. You can advance the relationship using automation rules. For example, at the end of the first email you send out, include a link at the bottom of the email that invites them to get a weekly tip, tool or resource. When they click on the link, they are automatically added to the next list, without having to go through the hassle of entering their name and email address again.

3. Internal Co-Reg or "Additional Interests"

If your optin form tells them they're going to get a report, deliver the report and ASK for permission to send them related offers or your weekly newsletter. Where you CAN generally mail again is if you are sending out another similar type of report, whitepaper, etc. But, what you should NOT do is send them offers about other topics.

TIP: Consider a confirmation page after they optin that invites them to sign up for other emails/offers. Think in terms of a "co-reg" model. For example, let's pretend we're in the "how to make money online" business. This opens the doors for a number of different types of offers, but someone is coming into your list for a specific reason initially. Here's a sample funnel that you could follow that would open the door to multiple types of offers:

- Optin form: Free social media checklist (send via email to ensure a real email address)

- Thank you page: A checklist of other types of offers/newsletters that they might be interested such as "Online Traffic Newsletter," "E-Commerce Reports," "Email Marketing," etc. Then, they simply check the boxes for the other types of offers they'd like to receive. They are then giving you permission to contact them about other types of offers. This allows them to segment themselves for additional offers that you may want to send out.

TIP: Use a different from name or a prefix in your subject lines to differentiate the different communication streams. Marketing Sherpa does this very well. When you sign up for their main newsletter, they give you the option of signing up for several others. When they come to your inbox, they are labeled as such. For example: Marketing Sherpa, Email Sherpa, and so on.

Another benefit of this model is that you can actually send multiple emails on the same day to the same subscriber if they've asked for them.

4. Offer a "Downsell"

We covered this in a bit of detail in chapter 3, but it is worth mentioning again briefly here.

Let's say that you're guilty of possibly "over mailing"... Moving forward, offer a downsell option that allows subscribers to change the frequency of emails. In other words, offer them a way to stop getting your daily email, but still receive the weekly "roundup."

At the end of the day, not only is it simple to set up a system that respects your subscribers' requests and still allows you to monetize your list on a regular basis. It just takes a bit of planning and preparation up front.

Not only will it help build a better relationship with your subscribers, but it will increase your engagement rate, increase your response rate, and decrease opt-outs and complaints. You'll make more money from your list and have happier subscribers. Plus, you'll have a well-segmented list that makes it easy to target specifically.

To recap, at the end of the day, it comes down to setting expectations and sticking with the expectations that were set at the beginning of the relationship. When all is said and done, it comes down to giving your subscribers what they expect out of the relationship.

5 Key Chapter Takeaways

1. Establish a "relationship" with your subscribers

2. Set expectations up front... *and stick to what you promise.* Permission to send a single item does not translate into permission to blast them daily

3. Create funnels that allow subscribers to move through your sequences seamlessly

4. Invite people to sign up for multiple types of offers by using an internal co-reg on the thank you page

5. Always offer a way for people to opt "down" for less frequent messages or specific types of emails only.

In the next chapter, we're going to go over how to maximize your email program for mobile subscribers.

Mistake #11: Not Optimizing Your Email Campaigns for Mobile

Just when marketers got comfortable with using HTML in their emails, mobile comes along and changes the game again!

This leads to a whole host of challenges for email marketers. It was hard enough when you just had to design your emails to work with different browsers and different mail clients. Add to that all the different phones and tablets, and it can be a wee bit overwhelming to say the least.

But here's the truth... Like it or not, mobile is here - *and it's not going anywhere!* In fact, according to Litmus, 47% of email is now opened on a mobile device. - *"Email Analytics" (April 2014)*

As much as you might want to, you can't keep your head in the sand and hope it all goes away. So, now is the time to start optimizing for mobile. That includes making sure your emails AND your landing pages are designed for mobile. You've got to work through the mobile "experience." If not, you're going to be leaving hundreds, thousands, even tens of thousands of dollars on the table.

In fact, a member in one of my mastermind groups was just talking about how much money he was losing simply because more and more of his subscribers were opening emails on their phones and not watching a full length VSLs (video sales letters) or reading a long form sales page. And once they've already read the email on their mobile, there's a high chance they're not going to come back to it when they get back to their computer.

The good news is that it's never too late to start! And it's getting easier and easier to do so with the plugins, resources, and tools available to you.

PLUS... there's a really good chance that your competitors aren't optimizing for mobile, so you'll separate yourself from the competition, relatively easily!

What's the Big Deal?

When it comes to reading emails - and clicking through to landing pages - on mobile devices, the user experience is frustrating in many cases. Buttons are small, font is small, and the text is often broken up on different lines, making it difficult to read.

People have to enlarge the screen and scroll up and down and side to side to even read your message (and that's BEFORE they even click the link to get to the landing page)!

If they do actually click through, they're greeted with:

- An optin form that's hard to fill in (it's either too small, requires scrolling, or has too many fields)

- A video that they may not have time (or desire) to watch right now

- A long sales letter that is simply too difficult to read on their device

So, even if your subscribers DO click through, they're likely to close the window and go back to their email to continue checking messages.

Optimizing Your Campaigns for Mobile

Here are 7 things you can start doing immediately to improve the mobile experience for your subscribers:

1. Gather statistics

It's important to start tracking where your subscribers are reading your messages.

2. Pay Attention to Message Length

Shorter emails perform better on mobile than long copy. People are more inclined to read longer, more detailed email messages on a desktop device than they are on an iPhone. So, if the majority of your subscribers are reading your emails on their phones, then consider making your emails shorter, with the most compelling and important content at the top of the email. At the very least, if you're not tracking devices, test different types (and lengths) of your messaging.

3. Test Number of Columns

There are different schools of thought on whether a single column layout or two column is better. Traditionally, marketers have been told that single column works best, but several research studies show that 2 or 3 column layouts might perform better because people are accustomed to zooming to read text. With a single column, readers may have to scroll left to right whereas with multiple columns, they can zoom in and easily read the text without left to right scrolling.

4. Use A Reply-To Mechanism or Auto-Register

Since it's more difficult to interact on a mobile device, consider asking people to interact by replying to the message directly. With most email clients, you can modify the "reply to" email address. In other words, they can hit reply to be added to the product launch update list. Another option is to automatically sign up for a webinar or teleseminar by clicking a link in the email. So instead of having to enter their details, you automatically register them. You obviously have their email address if you sent them the invite, so why ask for it again when you can instantly subscribe them?

5. Grab Attention with Your Subject Line & Pre-head

You have fewer characters to get the open, so be sure to craft a powerful subject line. Don't forget about the pre-head. Different devices and clients will have different displays, but most will have some sort of preview text that can also help with the open.

6. Use Responsive (or Scalable) Email Design

Scalable design uses one layout that scales well across all devices. It may be full size on a desktop and then shrinks down on your phone. It looks good on desktop devices and mobile devices and the user simply has to zoom in and out to read the message. Responsive design, on the other hand, uses CSS3 and media queries to determine how to display the content. For example, you may determine that if the display is less than 480px, show one version whereas if it larger, show another version.

NOTE: There are certain environments that don't work well/support media queries, so you'll want to keep that in mind when making a decision on which type of design to go with.

7. Don't Forget About Your Landing Page(s)

It's one thing to make the email readable on the device. It's another to actually have a successful experience for the subscriber (and to generate your desired response). Take time to consider the experience and optimize accordingly. At the very least, use a mobile redirect. This is just simple code that goes on your website that looks at the device and makes a decision as to what version to display.

While this means creating/maintaining 2 versions, the results will be well worth the effort.

To make this simple, visit: http://detectmobilebrowsers.com. You can choose a number of different languages depending on what your site is built on. All you need to do is:

1. Download the file

2. Edit it to include your mobile URL

3. Upload the file to your server

4. Add the javascript code in your header tag

(If this sounds confusing, don't worry! Send it off to your webmaster to take care of it for you!)

BONUS TIP: Test, Test, Test!

This goes without saying... but all too often, marketers are in a rush and don't take the time to test. Ideally, you'll find - or create - some templates that you know work, and can use over and over again. But even if that's the case, you want to test periodically since things change quickly when it comes to technology, so what looked great 6 months ago, may no longer be supported.

If you follow the recommendations above, you'll find that it's actually quite easy to optimize for mobile, and the results will speak for themselves.

The good news is that if you do follow these steps, you'll be ahead of your competitors instantly. It doesn't have to be complicated... It just takes a little extra planning and preparation, but it will pay off big time in the long run.

To recap, mobile is here and it's not going anywhere any time soon, so it's important to start integrating a mobile strategy into your email program.

1. 47% of email is now opened on a mobile device. - Litmus, "Email Analytics" (April 2014).

2. Design for mobile devices in order to increase responsiveness with your emails.

3. Create a standard template for your messages (responsive vs. scalable design).

4. Optimize your landing page for mobile.

5. Test regularly as technology is always changing and what worked one day may not work the next.

In the next chapter, we're going to cover the technical side of emails including authentication and feedback loops. We saved this until last so you could simply hand it along to your technical person after you have a chance to read through it!

Mistake #12: Not having the right infrastructure in place

There's a good chance that you're going to want to skip right over this chapter. This is the reason we put this chapter towards the end of the book!

Some of it is probably going to sound like gobbledygook and you probably want to read this about as much as you'd like to hear nails clawing on a chalkboard. BUT... There are some basic things that need to be in place before you send your first email.

I encourage you to at least skim over the information or, better yet, hand it off to your technical team.

Also, a good bit of this may not apply to you if you're using a shared IP email service provider (we discussed this in Chapter 2), but it is important to understand it so that you can hold your ESP accountable in the event that something goes wrong. Plus, there are a few things that will still apply to you even if you're using an email service that claims to handle it all for you.

If you don't have the foundation in place, nothing else that we discussed in the rest of this book is going to matter.

The catch here is that there's a good chance you've never even heard of many of the things we're going to cover. In fact, just a few years ago, I was in your shoes... And I had to learn it the hard way, as I went!

Basically, back in 2005, I began seeing a decline in my sales and I was not sure what to do with my business. I was about to close the doors when a friend of mine suggested that I may not have a business model problem, but rather an email problem.

So, before I threw out the baby with the bathwater, I decided to give it a shot.

I installed a piece of software on my server, exported all of my contacts from my previous provider and began sending. I started instantly getting messages from subscribers who thought I was out of the business. It turns out that many of my subscribers hadn't gotten a message from me in more than 6 months even though my service provider showed I was sending these messages out every single week.

The very next month, my sales increased nearly 600%. Nothing changed other than how I was sending my email.

All was well... until it wasn't!

I got a message that might as well have been written in Chinese. It basically told me that my emails were getting blocked and if I wanted to fix it, I would have to fill out this form, which was a page and a half long, asking for about 30 things I couldn't answer.

My answer to that was simply to start over... a new domain and a new IP address!

That worked for a little while, but then that stopped working and it was time to get it right and stop playing whack-a-mole!

So at that time, I went ahead and took the time to painfully learn about all of the moving parts, which continue to be moving targets.

NOTE: The email game changes quickly and you've got to be on top of it.

So What Are the Pieces of the Puzzle You Need to Know

This is the part that I'd hand over to your system admin, server admin, or similar! There are some basic things that you'll need to have in place. Most, if not all, of these items should be taken care of as part of your service or during your setup if you're using a boutique service, like EmailDelivered, to manage your email program.

- SPF

- DKIM (domain keys identified mail)

- domainkeys

- SenderID

- DMARC

SPF

SPF, quite simply, tells whether or not a domain is allowed to send over a particular IP address. In other words, xyz.com is allowed to send email through IP address 10.20.30.40. You'll want to set this for any "from" domains you want to use to send email. Ask your ESP what to put in your SPF records if you're using a service. This is handled in the DNS zone for your domain, so this is something you will need to do at your registrar, hosting provider, or wherever you are hosting DNS for the domains you are using in your from address.

Aside from being a minimum requirement for delivery to the ISPs, a domain that publishes an SPF record is less like to be used by spammers and phishers. As a result, it's less likely to be blacklisted by spam filters, getting more legitimate email through.

To learn more about SPF, visit: http://www.openspf.org/

NOTE: SPF is one of the pieces that you may need to handle even if you're using an email service provider. The more reputable providers will provide you with SPF records so that you can add them to any domains from which you will be sending.

DKIM

DKIM stands for domain keys identified mail and this has largely replaced domainkeys in the recent years. It is a method to prevent spammers from faking an email identity. DKIM is a digital signature that proves your identity by identifying the "domain" part of the sending address and verifies that the message is actually coming from the right source.

To read more about DKIM, visit http://www.DKIM.org

Domainkeys

Domainkeys was developed by Yahoo over a decade ago and has since been deprecated. It's not a bad idea to use it as well as DKIM, but it has largely been replaced by DKIM across the board.

SenderID

SenderID is similar to SPF. It was developed - and is primarily used by - Microsoft (Hotmail/MSN/Outlook). It verifies the IP address of the sender against the sending domain. This helps mainly with email going to addresses managed by Microsoft.

To setup SenderID, you can use the Wizard provided by Microsoft: http://www.microsoft.com/mscorp/safety/content/technologies/senderid/wizard

DMARC

DMARC stands for "Domain-based Message Authentication, Reporting & Conformance." It was developed by a group of contributors including Google, ReturnPath, Microsoft, Yahoo, AOL and others, to name a few and it is relatively new although more and more companies are implementing DMARC weekly.

DMARC allows a sender to state that their emails are protected by SPF and/or DKIM (see above) and tells the receiver what to do if the authentication method fails. For example, it may direct the recipient to reject the message. DMARC also provides a mechanism for the recipient to report back to the sender for review.

To learn more about DMARC, visit: http://www.dmarc.org/

But Wait! There's More!

The items we touched on briefly above are kind of like the foundation on your house. If those aren't in place, nothing else that we talked about will matter. It will come crashing down around you. Your IPs and domains will get blacklisted. Your messages will get blocked.

But before we tie up this chapter, there's one more piece of this "foundation" puzzle we need to cover and that is "Feedback Loops."

Feedback Loops

Feedback Loops (FBL), also known as "complaint feedback loops," are essentially just a notification from an ISP or mailbox provider that one of their customers has clicked the "spam" button. Feedback loops are one of the primary ways subscribers can report spam and it is often easier for subscribers to hit the spam button rather than go through the unsubscribe process (**TIP:** Make it easy to unsubscribe to reduce complaints).

Once you have set up your feedback loops, the ISP will send you an email every time someone clicks the spam button. You should then remove those people from your list immediately and cease sending those addresses further messages.

NOTE: Whether or not - and how to - provide a FBL is a choice of the mailbox provider. Not all providers have this mechanism in place, but the majority of the major ones do.

The current feedback loops that you can apply for include:

- AOL - http://www.postmaster.aol.com/Postmaster.FeedbackLoop.html

- Bluetie/Excite - http://feedback.bluetie.com

- Comcast - http://feedback.comcast.net

- Cox - http://fbl.cox.net

- Earthlink (email only)

- Fastmail - http://fbl.fastmail.fm

- Hotmail - https://support.msn.com/eform.aspx?productKey=edfsjmrpp&page=support_home_options_form_byemail&ct=eformts&scrx=1

- OpenSRS/Tucows - http://fbl.hostedemail.com

- Rackspace (formerly Mailtrust) - http://fbl.apps.rackspace.com

- RoadRunner/Time Warner Cable - http://feedback.postmaster.rr.com

- Synacor - http://fbl.synacor.com

- USA.NET - http://fbl.usa.net

- United Online/Juno/Netzero - http://www.unitedonline.net/postmaster/whitelisted.html

- Yahoo! - http://feedbackloop.yahoo.net (requires DomainKeys or DKIM)

You'll want to set this up BEFORE you begin mailing from your new IPs. Often times, when you start mailing from a new environment, your deliverability will increase substantially. Consequently, people that had not been receiving your emails previously are now getting them. That's good news except for the fact that, depending on how long they haven't been receiving your emails, they may have forgotten they signed up for your emails and hit the spam button.

We typically see an increase in spam complaints for the first 30 days when clients first start sending from EmailDelivered. This is simply due to the fact that their emails either weren't getting delivered or were going to the spam folder.

If all of this completely overwhelms you - or bores you to tears - don't worry! Contact http://EmailDelivered.com/Assessment to run an audit on your email program and let you know where the holes in your program are.

If you don't want to do any of this "stuff," EmailDelivered can take care of all of this, so you can do what you do best: market to your subscribers!

To recap... Don't get overwhelmed by the items discussed in this chapter. It's important to at least have a basic understanding of email authentication so you can hand it off to your tech team.

1. Email changes rapidly, so it's important to stay on top of the technology.

2. Your email infrastructure is critical to your success and it must be setup properly from the beginning.

3. Even if you're using an email service provider (ESP), you should be familiar with SPF as many will require you to add their IP(s) to your domain.

4. Ensure that feedback loops are setup for all the ISPs that offer them, and remove complainers immediately.

5. If this is overwhelming to you, and you prefer to hand it over, get a free email assessment at http://EmailDelivered.com/Assessment.

In the next section, we'll tie things together so you can take action on the things we discussed throughout this book.

Final Thoughts & Next Steps...

Now that we've covered all the "details", it's time to take action. It's great to have the knowledge, but without some sort of action, the information is only going to frustrate you because once the cat is out of the bag, you can't put it back in.

You're likely going to question your current email program and wonder if your deliverability or your inbox placement rates are what your email provider is telling you. You're likely to have LOTS of questions, and that's good. You'll be able to ask the right questions and make the right decisions moving forward with your business.

Start by auditing your current email program to see where the holes may be and what to start working on. You can either do this yourself or have an "Email Marketing Audit" run for you at EmailDelivered.

Once you have identified the holes, start plugging them one by one.

Some of the suggestions may be as simple as changing the frequency of which you are sending emails or perhaps starting a weekly ezine that goes out to subscribers. These types of fixes take just a few minutes. There are other fixes, such as setting up dedicated resources, which may take more time and planning to execute.

It's also important to remember not to get bogged down by all the "technical" details. There are people that can take care of those pieces for you. All you need to know is what to tell them to do (and verify they've done it).

Let's quickly summarize the key takeaways from each of the chapters that we discussed so you have a cheat sheet of sorts. Then, when you're ready to tackle a particular mistake, you can simply look here and then go back and find the details in the actual chapter.

Chapter #1:

Mistake: Not Knowing What Your Email Reputation Is (Reputation is Everything!)

5 Key Takeaways

1. Everyone has a specific email reputation and it's important to monitor yours regularly and keep it as clean as possible.

2. The top factors that impact your email reputation are general setup/configuration, list quality, spam traps, complaints/complaint rate, and message content.

3. If you're using an ESP (email service provider), you're most likely sharing the IP address with other senders.

4. Not all domains are visible in your emails. It's important to know - and test - all the domains in your emails (and your headers).

5. Messages don't just "disappear". Generally, when a message seems to vanish, it is due to a problem with the reputation.

Chapter #2:

Mistake: Using Shared IP Addresses to Send Your Email (You're Only As Good as the Weakest Link)

5 Key Takeaways

1. Most email service providers use shared IP addresses (if you DO have a dedicated IP with an ESP, then it's

important to make sure they're managing the reputation).

2. When you're sending through shared IP addresses, you are only as good as the weakest link.

3. Dedicated IP addresses give you more control over your email program.

4. Consider getting a dedicated IP address on your own server or via an SMTP relay service that understands the complexities of email marketing, like EmailDelivered.com.

5. Be sure you have all the "technical pieces" in place before you start sending out of our own IP.

Chapter #3:

Mistake: Not Testing Message Content

5 Key Takeaways

1. Content is one of the key reasons that email messages wind up in the spam folder, and it's the single easiest component that you can control, regardless of your email service provider.

2. Don't try to be sneaky with buzzwords like free or money. A single word or phrase is not likely to cause your message to get sent to spam.

3. Always test your messages in each of the email clients before sending (and edit the content, if necessary, until the message inboxes).

4. Check the domains in your emails against blacklists to ensure that the tracking domains as well as the landing domains do not have a poor reputation.

5. Verify your HTML formatting is correct using a service like Litmus.com or EmailOnAcid.com

Chapter 4

Mistake #4: Not addressing high complaint rates

1. Complaints occur when subscribers hit the spam button instead of unsubscribing naturally from your list.

2. Too many spam complaints can cause your ESP to shut you down OR cause deliverability problems (if you're using a dedicated solution).

3. High spam complaints can indicate a few potential issues including (1) lack of consistency, (2) too much email, (3) the wrong type(s) of messages, or (4) an indicator your previous ESP was not getting emails delivered to the inbox.

4. Make it easy for people to unsubscribe. Do not require extra steps or hoops for them to jump through.

5. Use your complaints to identify problems and improve your email program.

Chapter 5

Mistake #5: Doing the Same Thing Over & Over and Expecting Different Results (Not Running Re-Engagement Campaigns or Segmenting Your Subscribers)

1. Segment your list. If you've not already been segmenting, it's never too late to start. Create some surveys to collect data that you can use in your marketing in exchange for a special bonus gift.

2. Gather as much information about your subscribers as possible over time (including subscriber-stated preferences AND behaviors).

3. Run re-engagements regularly to clean out the dead weight.

4. Remove unengaged subscribers between 90 - 180 days depending on your strategy (or at the very least, downgrade their email frequency).

5. Let subscribers manage their own preferences.

Chapter #6

Mistake #6: Using Affiliate Swipe Copy "As-Is"

5 Key Takeaways

1. Using affiliate swipe copy "as is" can not only cause your promotional emails to wind up in the spam folder, but can also impact your long term email deliverability.

2. Always use the same voice when communicating with your list (which means you need to rewrite swipe copy in your own voice 100% of the time).

3. Personalized endorsements almost always outperform any other type of affiliate promotion.

4. When participating in product launches, consider using intermediate landing pages to pre-frame/pre-sell the reader.

5. Be very careful when promoting products from affiliate networks.

Chapter 7

Mistake #7: Email Until They Die or Buy

5 Key Takeaways

1. Gone are the days where you can just continue to email over and over and over again until the person drops off one way or another.

2. It's important to pay attention to the bounce messages you receive from the ISPs and take regular action.

3. Run frequent re-engagement campaigns to try to recapture people that haven't been "listening" for some time (consider 90 - 180 days to start).

4. Take un-engaged subscribers and run a Facebook targeting campaign to try and offer them something related to the original offer/reason they signed up with you in the first place.

5. Finally, consider running a data append to your list and getting phone numbers and mailing addresses to follow up with different media.

Chapter 8

Mistake #8: Buying, Renting, Trading or Scraping Email Addresses

1. Buying, renting, or trading email lists (or scraping) is almost always a losing model, regardless of how good your marketing is to try to warm them up.

2. Using "shortcuts" to build your list will damage your email reputation and can potentially impact your deliverability for your current subscribers.

3. Most email service providers and web hosts have strong policies regarding bulk email and list building. Engaging in these strategies may cause your account to be suspended or, worse, terminated without notice.

4. There are lots of valid ways to build a loyal subscriber base that don't have to cost a lot of money.

5. Consider using a combination of list building strategies including social media to re-engage unengaged subscribers, recapture unsubscribed leads, and warm up cold lists.

Chapter #9

Mistake #9: Not Providing A Balance of Content and Sales Messages

5 Key Takeaways

1. Always provide value to your subscribers.

2. Remember that your subscribers are real people and not just a digital cash machine (foster the RELATIONSHIP).

3. Incorporate both selling and content into your email. No sales = no money. No content = no subscribers! Both are equally important.

4. Use a promotional calendar to ensure that you are giving great content and that your overall messaging flows.

5. Balance content and sales into a ratio that works for you, 50/50 at a minimum.

Chapter 10

Mistake #10: Not Respecting the Relationship

1. Establish a "relationship" with your subscribers.

2. Set expectations up front... *and stick to what you promise.* Permission to send a single item does not translate into permission to blast them daily.

3. Create funnels that allow subscribers to move through your sequences seamlessly.

4. Invite people to sign up for multiple types of offers by using an internal co-reg on the thank you page.

5. Always offer a way for people to opt "down" for less frequent messages or specific types of emails only.

Chapter 11

Mistake #11: Not Optimizing Your Email Campaigns for Mobile

1. 47% of email is now opened on a mobile device. - Litmus, "Email Analytics" (April 2014).

2. Design for mobile devices in order to increase responsiveness with your emails.

3. Create a standard template for your messages (responsive vs. scalable design).

4. Optimize your landing page for mobile.

5. Test regularly as technology is always changing and what worked one day may not work the next.

Chapter #12

Mistake #12: Not having the right infrastructure in place

5 Key Takeaways

1. Email changes rapidly, so it's important to stay on top of the technology.

2. Your email infrastructure is critical to your success and it must be setup properly from the beginning.

3. Even if you're using an email service provider (ESP), you should be familiar with SPF as many will require you to add their IP(s) to your domain.

4. Ensure that feedback loops are setup for all the ISPs that offer them, and remove complainers immediately.

5. Get a free email assessment at http://EmailDelivered.com/Assessment.

Don't Get Left Behind

Your Personal Invitation from Heather Seitz...

Now that you've finished reading "The Experts Guide to Email Marketing: How to Avoid the Top 12 Email Marketing Mistakes That Prevent Your Emails from Getting to the Inbox," you know many of the components to a successful email program. If you don't have the time, the experience, or the desire to evaluate your current email program to determine where to make changes, we're offering you a free email marketing audit.

The fact that you've gotten this far shows that you're serious about your email program and want to have a bigger, more responsive list that opens your messages, clicks on your links, and buys your products and services.

I'd like to invite you to get your own Email Marketing Audit, where my team will go through your email program and show you which of these mistakes you may be making and how to correct them. As added value, we'll also add you to our weekly "Email Delivered Tips" Newsletter that shares with you the latest information on email marketing and email deliverability as we learn about it.

If you want to identify potential problems in your program, increase your open rates and click through rates, and increase your sales through email marketing, then here's what I'd like to invite you to do.

Go ahead and logon to **www.EmailDelivered.com/audit** and sign up for a free audit. It takes about 60 seconds and will save you time and money, and will keep you from continuing to play the guessing game with your email marketing. This could be the single best business decision you make all year.

Again, signing up is easy and the audit is FREE for people that purchased this book. Just go to **www.EmailDelivered.com/audit** and sign up for a free account. We promise not to spam you or share your information with anyone...

So, if you enjoyed this book and want to get more opens, clicks and sales from your email marketing, then head on over to www.EmailDelivered.com/audit right now and get onboard for free.

Bonus Report: Email Marketing and Deliverability 101

First things first... Email Marketing is Alive and Well!

There are so many folks out there touting the death of email marketing and the total takeover of social media as the only vehicle to get your message out to the masses.

Now, there are other contributors in this book that are far more qualified to talk about social media than I am, so I will leave that to the experts, but what I will say is simply that social media has not killed email marketing. In fact, there's a direct link to how much email one consumes based on how engaged they are with social media (i.e. the more folks use social media, the more they use email!).

So now that that's out of the way... let's get into the ins and outs of email marketing in the current economy!

There are essentially 3 components when it comes to email marketing:

1. List Building

2. Marketing

3. Deliverability

List Building

There are "right" and "wrong" ways to build your list and it's important to understand both sides of the coin so you can avoid costly mistakes that can hurt you in the long term.

To properly build your list, there are 3 components:

1. Lead Capture Mechanism

2. Ability to Capture Email Addresses

3. Email Follow Up Sequence

Let's go through each of these:

1. Lead Capture Mechanism

There are several ways that you can capture "leads" depending on your unique business.

For example, if you're a restaurant or a retail store, you should have the customer fill out a form with their contact information including Name, Email Address, Cell phone number with permission to text (if they are willing to do so), and Birthday, for example (if you want to offer special deals for their birthday).

If you're an online business, then you'll need a web page on your website that allows subscribers to fill out a simple form with their basic information. The key here is to give them a compelling reason to trade you their name and email address. Remember, NOBODY wants any more junk mail!

Consider giving them a special report with weekly updates in exchange for their email address. Only you know your ideal customer, so you'll need to think of something that has high value for your audience and give it to them for free. The only "strings" are that they need to provide you with a valid email address (more on how to verify that they're giving you a real address later).

TIP: The less information you ask for, the more people will sign up for your newsletter, special promotions, etc. If you want to capture more than a name and email, consider doing that as part of a 2-step process.

2. Ability to Capture Email Addresses

Once someone is willing to give you their email address, you need a place to collect that information so that you can actually USE it to generate more sales, increase your bottom line, and create loyal customers.

We're not talking a "Google Spreadsheet" or an "Excel Sheet" here that an employee enters in all the new forms that you received in the past 24 hours.

Likewise, your teenage nephew can probably create a simple web form for you that emails you every person that comes to your website and fills out a form, but that's not going to do you much good either.

You need actual email software to be able to effectively use these addresses.

Don't let the word "software" scare you! You don't need to have any technical skills whatsoever. There are dozens of online services that handle all the "technical" stuff for you.

The key is to find a service that allows you to send BOTH:

1. Pre-programmed sequential emails; and

2. Group broadcasts (or promotions)

If you don't already have email software, consider "Constant Contact" or "Mail Chimp." Constant Contact has a 60 day trial and Mail Chimp allows you a number of contact free for the life of the account with some restrictions.

They both have easy to use tutorials that will get forms onto your websites in just a matter of minutes.

And, if you're entering the data yourself (or have a staff member doing so), you can enter each record into their database or upload a file all at once if you have it in digital format already.

3. Email Follow Up Sequence (Optional, but Recommended)

An automated follow up sequence, or autoresponder series, is optional, but makes sense for most businesses, especially when you're collecting leads from your website.

Your autoresponder series should accomplish the following:

- Build trust and credibility with the prospect or customer

- Establish some "ground rules"

- Get them to spend some money (or more money) with you

It doesn't have to be long or complicated. It can simply be 3-5 email messages that are preprogrammed.

Here's a basic sequence you may consider using:

NOTE: This sequence is designed to trigger as soon as the person is added to the email software regardless of whether the customer/prospect entered his or her information or if you did.

Immediately: "Welcome to {Your Company, Newsletter Name, Brand, etc.}"

This email would welcome the subscriber to your "special offers" club, to your newsletter, or to your updates. This simply depends on what your particular business is.

For example, if you were a retail store, it might say something like: "Welcome to 'Your Stores' Hot Deals" (Assuming you send coupons or in-store deals to your subscribers).

Or if you were a cookie gift box company, it might say something like: "Welcome to Carrie's Cookie Club"

If you're an online business, the subject of your welcome email might be: "Welcome to The Magic Bean Marketing Newsletter: Issue #1"

This email should also set the expectation. In other words, let your subscribers now what types of emails they should expect to get from you and how frequently.

1-2 Days Later: "Special gift or offer"

Several days after your initial email, it's time to send your new subscribers a special offer. This could be a coupon to get them INTO your physical location (i.e. a free appetizer or cocktail), or a special intro offer to your product or service (think "Groupon").

The thing to remember here, however, is that you must put a deadline on this.

This is designed to engage your new subscribers in spending money with you, and to help them become long-term customers. You want to give them a great reason to do business with you.

And... you'll want to make certain that you have a flawless first experience.

That means, if you've got a storefront, that you have friendly staff that are professional and attentive... If you're a restaurant, that the food is impeccable and the service extraordinary... If you're a photography studio, the photos capture the emotion of the subject... If you're an online info business, you provide great customer support, follow up with a phone call, and provide a stellar product... and so on!

This is the time to "hook" them and bring them into your business and experience the best of what you have to offer.

Remember the saying: you never get a chance to make a first impression!

2-3 Days Later: "Follow Up"

The biggest mistake that most entrepreneurs, business owners, and online marketers make is that they don't implement deadline-driven promotions and follow up.

So, 2-3 days later, it's time to follow up and remind them of this special offer – or gift – and let them know it's expiring. Most people nowadays are motivated to act by deadlines. So, you've got to condition your folks to take action when you present offers.

2-3 Days Later: "Other Stuff"

All of us have different products, services, and value that we bring to our customers. Most of our customers are only aware of a very small sliver of those offerings.

This is a great time to introduce these new subscribers to other "stuff" you have to offer.

For example, if you're an information marketer, you might want to let subscribers know about other products or services that you have. Perhaps you run frequent webinars, have a coaching program, or have a large product line that they're not aware of.

If you're a photographer and you had a client come in for wedding photos, perhaps you also photograph memorable photos for Christmas cards, or have a special niche for babies.

If you're a restaurant, be sure to let customers know that you can host special events, happy hours, etc.

2-3 Days Later - Invite Feedback: "What Do YOU Want?"

This is the time to let your subscribers tell you what they want. This can give you some great ideas, some new insight on what your customers are looking for, and more. Many email services offer "surveys" or "feedback forms" as part of the service, so don't worry about the technical stuff.

If you don't have an "automated" way to capture feedback (i.e. surveys), then you can simply tell them to email you at feedback@yourwebsite.com or to visit your Twitter feed or Facebook page and send a link to the topic that opens the door for feedback.

No Facebook or Twitter account? No worries... There are some excellent resources in this very report that will get you up and running there in a snap (literally a few minutes!).

Additional Emails:

You can add unlimited email messages to your automated sequence. Anything that you can send to your subscribers 365 days per year could be added to your autoresponder series.

Think about it as a perpetual cash machine!

All you've got to do is write it once, add it to the sequence, and it lives forever ;-)

This is phase one of your email campaign. And I can tell you with 100% certainty that if you take these steps and get a lead capture system in place with an autoresponder follow up series, you WILL increase your revenue. PERIOD.

And the best part is... you've only got to do it ONCE!

TIP: If you need ideas for promotions or autoresponders, visit www.EmailMessageWizard.com for push button wizards that write 90% of the messages for you with a few clicks of a mouse!

REMEMBER, the first step is to get a system in place for capturing leads!

Now that you've got Phase I in place, you're ready to kick it up a notch!

This is where Email Marketing pays BIG TIME! It can literally provide you with unlimited returns since it is so CHEAP to use.

Let's just look at what this can mean to your bottom line...

Scenario #1: Bricks and Mortar Store

The lead capture part is easy here and it's essentially FREE. Your only expense is the toner and paper you use to print the sign up forms.

TIP: Hire it out to a local printer who can print them for you on mini custom notepads. Depending on the volume, you can get them done for you for pennies/page!

Customers fill out the form with their information and you simply enter it into your database... (Remember, as soon as you enter the person into your database, it fires off the first email in the autoresponder and follows up automatically).

Let's just say 1 in 10 people comes back into your store in the next 14 days to buy something and that the average profit is $20.

If you get 25 people in a 7-day period to fill out their information, that's an extra $50 profit in a week. I realize that's not going to make you retire tomorrow. However, what if you systematize this to get every single customer to fill out one of these? What if you get 100 people per week? That's another $200/week or another $10,400 per year towards your bottom line.

And remember... that's just the very FIRST sale! It doesn't take into account additional promotions OR the people you've added to your database over the course of a year!

Let's say just 20% of THOSE folks come back in one additional time because of an email promotion you sent them. It's literally FREE money that you wouldn't have seen any other way!

NOTE: These are very LOW numbers in this scenario because you're capturing people who have already come into your store, studio, restaurant, etc. They've already SPENT money with you, so getting them to do it again is the easy part!

You can now send them emails over and over again until they unsubscribe from your list!

Scenario #2: Online Info Business

All you need here is a form to capture subscribers. It's free to set up less the cost of your webmaster to put the form on your site.

So let's say you're getting 100 visitors to your website a day and 25% of them sign up for your offer. That's 25 per day or 175 new subscribers/week. (These are both very low numbers).

The conversion rate is slightly lower for online leads since they don't have an existing relationship with you, but you can get more of them since you're not relying solely on customers walking into your physical location.

Let's say you get 10% of them to take you up on your killer offer. Let's say that your average profit is $25 per sale (remember to make it a killer offer for the first experience with you).

That's an EXTRA $22,100 per year on top of what you're already doing.

Plus… the benefit here is that you can offer upsells, easily engage subscribers with your other products and services very quickly, invite them to teleseminars or webinars, or cross-promote affiliate products and services.

Marketing

Now that you've gotten your initial sequence in place and have started adding people to your list, it's time to maximize your email program to generate additional revenue – virtually ON DEMAND!

NOTE: Promotion doesn't necessarily mean "sale". You could offer some special bonus or perk instead of a "discount". For example, if you're an auto repair shop, you could offer a free car wash with any service. If you're an accounting firm, perhaps you audit the last 3 years of tax returns free. If you're a fitness studio, consider offering a free nutrition workshop. If you're an info marketer, offer a Q&A follow up call. And so on!

There are essentially 3 "types" of promotions:

1. Holidays

2. Events

3. Subscriber-Centered

Let's look at each of these promotions and how you can use them in your business as a marketing tool to generate more business.

1. Holidays

Everybody loves holidays! The big box stores (i.e. Macy's, Target, even Amazon) always use these types of events to run special promotions and sales.

What does that mean to you?

Simply this: HOLIDAY PROMOTIONS WORK!

Why is it that "holiday" promotions are SO successful?

People are, by and large, procrastinators. They wait until the deadline is looming before they take action. If they know that they can come into your restaurant and get a free appetizer any day of the year, what's the reason they should come NOW?

Answer: NONE!

So, by using holidays as a reason to get people through the doors of your bricks and mortar business or to your online sales page, you get them to take action in a short window.

The other benefit of holiday promotions is that you very rarely have people that try to convince you to "extend" the offer or special deal. They're used to seeing sales that start and end on a specific date and time.

I mean... could you imagine walking into Macy's and saying, "I didn't see the insert in the paper until it was too late. Can you please give me the 50% discount anyways?"

It just doesn't happen!

Some of the common holidays with a handful of promotion ideas include:

- New Years Day (start the new year off right, new years resolutions, etc.)

- Valentines Day ("sweetheart deals", gift for your honey, date night, etc.)

- St. Patrick's Day ("It's your lucky day", "save some green", etc.)

- Tax Day ($10.40 deals, pay their taxes, "uncle sam wants you", etc.)

- Mother's Day ("thank you, mom!", "better than flowers or candy", etc.)

- 4th of July (celebrate your independence, honoring our forefathers, etc.)

- Veterans Day (support a charity like Wounded Warriors, thank veterans for their service, etc.)

- Halloween ("deals so good, they're scary", "trick or treat", etc.)

- Black Friday (killer discounts and deals, your own "doorbusters", etc.)

- Cyber Monday (free shipping, bundle discounts, free wrapping, etc.)

- Christmas (12 Days of Christmas, get $XX for yourself for every $XXX gift card you purchase for someone else, etc.)

- And so on!

The thing about these holidays is they're tried and true! Retailers have been using these holidays as a "reason" to promote for decades!

You should be using these in both your email marketing as well as in your other marketing channels (i.e. flyers, radio ads, TV spots, etc.).

Generally a "holiday" promotion will consist of 2-4 emails. Certainly, in some cases you may have more, but never less than two.

Here's an example of a concept for a promotion around "Tax Day" (April 15th, 2015), which happens to fall on a Wednesday.

Thursday, April 9th: Subject: "Tax Day is Around the Corner"

Just a friendly reminder... time to get your taxes in by next Wednesday (or your extensions) if you're not quite ready!

Tell them what your tax day promotion is and have them "save the date"!

Monday, April 15th: Subject: "Don't Forget..."

If you're like millions of folks who spent the weekend getting their taxes together, it's time to reward yourself!

Go on to explain what your business is offering for "tax day"!

TIP: Schedule this to go out super early in the morning so it's in their inbox when they get to work first thing.

You can send 1-2 reminders between if you want to.

One of my favorite tax day promotions is one that McCormick and Schmick runs every year. They have a special menu on which everything is $10.40 on April 15th. We've been going out for that promotion every year for the last 4 or 5 years!

Before we move on to events, however, it's important to note that there is literally a holiday every single month, day and week of the year. They range from traditional holidays (like the ones above) to totally obscure and off the wall like:

- Rubber Ducky Day

- Ice Cream for Breakfast Day

- Grapefruit Month

- National Caffeine Awareness Month

- Act Happy Week

- And HUNDREDS More!

These "offbeat" holidays are great to inject some personality and some humor into your email promotions, so that your subscribers look forward to getting your emails... even if your ultimate intention is to get them to spend more money with your business.

Remember the old adage: People do business with people (and businesses) they know, like, and trust! This strategy is designed to help get your customers to LOVE you and look forward to hearing from you.

Now, you might be thinking: "I don't know how to write 'marketing' emails" or "I don't have time to write these promotions".

There several ways to do this:

1.   Hire an email copywriter to write a year's worth of promotions for you all at once. It might cost you a few dollars, but you'll have at least one promotion per month for an entire year!

2.   Watch your inbox for emails from other people and "swipe" their concepts (I did not say copy their content, but use the basic concept and come up with your own spin on it)

3.   Visit www.EmailMessageWizard.com for dozens of promotions where you simply enter your information, the concept for the promotion, click a button, and then

paste the campaign into your favorite email client with your edits, and bam... you're good to go!

2. Events

Events are simply that! There's "something" that occurs at a specific time. From a marketing standpoint, you've got 3 distinct windows of opportunity: before, during, and after the event.

An event may be a special happy hour you're hosting at your restaurant, an open house for your photography studio, a charity event that you co-sponsor with a local organization, a live teleseminar or webinar, a seminar or tradeshow, etc.

The reason events are such a great promotion strategy is because there is a specific date and time the event is going to happen. If the person shows up the day after, the event's over. PERIOD.

The length of time that you need to "promote" BEFORE an event depends on what the event itself is. For example, if you're hosting a teleseminar or webinar, then you may only need to promote a few days to a week in advance. However, if you're promoting for a charity event, you may need to start promoting months in advance.

Likewise, there's a limit to how much "post event" promotion you can do, but it depends somewhat on the actual event.

Here's an example of how you could use email to promote before, during, and after a teleseminar or webinar.

A teleseminar (another word for a "conference" call) – or webinar (a "conference call" with slides, images, or demonstration) – is extremely valuable for any business, but works especially well for online businesses, coaches and consultants, etc.

For this example, let's assume that you only do a teleseminar once every few months (this means you'll need a bit longer to promote it) and you'd like to do one this coming Thursday. If you do one every week, then the timeline would shorten quite a bit and/or you could skip the first few and simply start on Sunday or Monday.

Here are the concepts/subject lines that might work for you if you're an information marketer, speaker, author, coach, consultant, etc.

PRE EVENT:

10 Days Prior to the Teleseminar (Monday Before):
Subject: Free Teleseminar NEXT Thursday

This is just a quick intro to the event... Think of it like a "Save the Date"!

7 Days Prior to the Teleseminar (Thursday Before):
Subject: One week from today... Reserve your spot!

3 Days Prior to the Teleseminar (Monday Week of):
Subject: Here's what you'll learn THIS Thursday night...

Explain some of the benefits they'll get when they show up!

2 Days Prior to the Teleseminar (Tuesday Week of):
Subject: Should I Save Your Spot?

Day Before the Teleseminar (Wednesday Week of):
Subject: It Happens Tomorrow Night!

DURING EVENT:

Day of the Teleseminar (Day of the Event): Subject: Be on EARLY (The registration had been unbelievable!).

This implies scarcity!

You can also send a reminder via email or SMS (if they have given you permission to do so) to everyone that has registered a few minutes prior to getting started to remind them to get on the line.

BONUS TIP: If you have a partner or employee, you can continue to promote via social media while the webinar is going. Encourage attendees to post questions and comments on Twitter or FaceBook live!

POST EVENT:

Post event promotion is especially effective if you're "selling" something, which I absolutely recommend... even if it's just the recordings from the live event for $20!

In this particular scenario, you'd want to send an email out on Friday, Saturday, possibly Sunday, and Monday!

Day After the Teleseminar: Subject: Here's the Replay!

If you're "selling" the replay, then you might want to send out the notes from the teleseminar or something to that effect.

2 Days After the Teleseminar: Subject: Less Than 72 Hours!

Let them know the replay (or the special offer) is coming down in less than 72 hours – no exceptions! Tell them what they get when they purchase (features AND benefits).

3 Days After the Teleseminar: Subject: "Last Chance..." and/or "Surprise Bonus"

4 Days After the Teleseminar: Subject: It's GONE in less than 8 hours...

This is their final deadline to "purchase" whatever was offered as a result of the live event, to get bonuses for a donation, etc. It's best to send this around 3:00 – 4:00pm.

Any event would be similar in that you have an opportunity before, during, or after the event.

NOTE: Post event promotion is used primarily for enticing people to take action by a certain deadline. In our experience, when you're marketing a product or service on a live event, you can expect to get as many as 2 to 3 times the sales in the 4 days following the event than during the event itself.

3. Subscriber-Centered Promotions

Subscriber-centered promotions are promotions that are centered around your customers or prospects. These could include birthdays or anniversaries (their own or, for example, their 1 year anniversary as a member of your newsletter or VIP club).

Other subscriber-centered promotions could be related to past purchases, interests they've shared with you, and more.

Here are some ways to use subscriber-centered promotions:

Birthdays

- Offer a free dinner for the birthday person (they're going to most likely come with someone else – or multiple other people!) - Restaurant

- A free haircut or conditioning treatment if you come in the week of your birthday. - Salon

- Gift card good for a discount on any purchase during their birthday month. Specialty store

- 10 free photo cards with your favorite photograph from a recent shoot. Photography Studio

- Birthday discount code or a free item with purchase of another item. - Info Business

Anniversary (with a spouse or significant other)

- Free bottle of wine with your dinner. - Restaurant

- Free makeup application with hairstyle. – Salon

Past purchases

Think "Amazon" and how they give you recommendations based on things you've already purchased.

These types of promotions require a little more information from your subscribers and an email application that allows you to segment this data for promotions. However, they can pay off in a big way if you take the time to put them together.

The thing to remember is that you just need to get started! You don't need to roll out holiday promotions, special events and subscriber-centered promotions all at once.

Start with the holiday promotions and then add on to that. It's the fastest and easiest way to see an immediate impact in your business.

If you need help designing your own custom email program, contact us at: http://www.EmailMessageWizard.com.

Deliverability

The last component of your email program that we need to discuss is deliverability!

Now, don't worry! I'm not going to get all technical on you here, but there are some things that you need to be aware of to make sure you're getting the very best results possible with your campaigns.

You're investing time and (some) money into your email program, so you certainly want to make sure that it pays off for you!

There are a few things that can impact your deliverability and, as a result, the success of your email program.

Infrastructure

Assuming you are using a 3rd party service, the "infrastructure" piece of the puzzle should be handled for you, so there's not much to worry about there as long as you're using a reputable company.

Now, as you start to grow your database, you may want to look into bringing your email in house, but generally you would want to have at least 20,000 – 25,000 active subscribers (on the very LOW end) to consider this.

TIP: If you DO have 25,000+ subscribers and mail several times/week, then you may want to look at www.EmailDelivered.com.

If you're not running your own internal email program (which you shouldn't be if you don't have a very large list), the email service providers are not especially transparent with a lot of the information and metrics that you need to make sure you're running your program optimally.

Since the providers are not real clear on a lot of metrics, there are some things you can do to keep an eye on it internally, with the easiest being to create a seed list.

A seed list is just a list of internal email addresses that you check periodically to make sure messages are getting through to the major ISPs.

To do this:

1.   Set up a free email account at each of the major providers (Gmail, Hotmail/Outlook.com, Yahoo, and AOL).

2.   Add those email addresses to your database.

3.   Check to make sure your emails are making it to the inbox.

If not, then contact your email provider to fix the problem! If they won't (or can't), then find a new provider ;-)

Regarding deliverability, however, there are some things that you DO have some control over... These include:

Content

Content includes the email messages along with any and all links included in the messages. Most of the Email Service Providers out there don't give you much insight on when your messages are not getting delivered.

As a result, you'll want to take a few minutes to check your content PRIOR to sending it out in the first place.

Many email providers will have a spam-checking tool built right into the application. Just be sure to use it prior to sending your message and make any changes that need to be made PRIOR to sending.

Bad Addresses (Unknown Emails)

The email service providers are generally pretty good at getting these out of your list quickly. However, it's best not to have them at all!

So, if you're entering names that you've collected in a physical setting, be very careful to make sure the email addresses are added exactly as the person wrote them.

Spam Complaints

This is critical to pay attention to. The ISPs (like Gmail, Hotmail, AOL, Yahoo, etc.) are getting more and more strict when it comes to complaints. If you get too many, they'll start sending your email to the spam folder or, worse, rejecting it entirely. Not to mention... the company you use to send your email may shut you down for too many complaints.

For that reason alone... it's very important to pay attention to these. Your email company should be able to provide these statistics to you.

Now... you may be asking, "if someone has specifically signed up to receive my emails, why would they hit the spam button?"

That's a fair question!

The answer is simple... People are lazy and it's easier to hit the "spam" button in many cases rather than go through the unsubscribe process.

To limit spam complaints, be sure to send the type of emails that your subscribers signed up for, and the frequency in which they agreed to. In other words, if you said you were sending a weekly newsletter, but you start sending an email every day, you're going to tick a lot of people off.

You should also remove people that haven't responded to an email by opening the message or clicking on your links after 6 months.

Don't worry! Your email software will tell you who's who!

Assuming that you are using legitimate list building practices (i.e. not buying lists or scraping the web), you should NOT have a major issue with typical spam traps.

A typical, or "pristine" spam trap is an email address that does not – and has not – EVER belonged to a real human being. The sole purpose of the address is to catch "spammers". So, when building your list properly, this should not be an issue.

However, there is another kind of spam trap called a "recycled" spam trap. These are email addresses that used to belong to a person, but has since been abandoned and then "recycled" into a spam trap.

NOTE: abandoned addresses are not recycled for several months/even years in some cases.

These traps are designed to catch people that don't clean out their list!

Again, if you're using an email service provider, you should be in good shape here and have nothing to worry about. There are PLENTY of notifications (aka bounces) sent back that indicate the email address doesn't exist. Your email provider will automatically remove those for you.

If you're using your own hosted email solution (i.e. internal email solution), then you will need to pay attention to bounce reports and remove hard bounces immediately.

If you want to learn more about email deliverability, visit www.EmailDelivered.com where there are articles, blog posts and free reports on deliverability, inbox placement, and more...

Key Takeaways

- Email marketing is the single advertising and marketing vehicle that is virtually free and provides you with an unlimited return on investment.

- Collecting leads is simple and requires either a webform (for online businesses) or a paper form (for bricks and mortar businesses).

- When you're getting started, use a service like MailChimp.com or ConstantContact.com (they're VERY inexpensive and easy to use).

- NOTE: If you already have a large list, consider self-hosting your email and using a service like EmailDelivered.com to handle deliverability.

- Start by sending one "holiday" promotion per month. Once you've got that down, you can grow from there.

- Use EmailMessageWizard.com to help you write proven email promotions in minutes – even if you're a lousy writer or you're a total newbie when it comes to marketing!

Action Items

We've covered quite a bit here regarding email marketing, but the key is to get started. Don't worry about every detail that we've gone over. Here are 5 steps to get started today (in under 60 minutes).

1. Sign up for an email service.

2. Start collecting leads. (If you're a bricks and mortar store, print out sign up pages until you can order actual notepads. Dimensions 4.25 X 3.5 work well. If you're an online business, add a form to your website homepage).

3. Choose a holiday promotion (or other type of promotion) to send in the next 30 days. (Use www.EmailMessageWizard.com if you need help).

4. Program it into your email client. Set it and forget it!

Resources

Email Marketing Tips, Campaigns and Newsletters:

- www.EmailMessageWizard.com

Email Software:

- Contact us for recommendations or visit www.EmailDelivered.com/blog for reviews on different email software.

Email Deliverability Tips:

- www.EmailDelivered.com

Made in the USA
Lexington, KY
21 October 2014